WHITBY
WEST CLIFF STATION

WHITBY
WEST CLIFF STATION

MIKE HITCHES & PAUL HUGHES

AMBERLEY

West Cliff station in the early 1950s. A typical summer's day. (N. Cholmondeley collection)

First published 2011

Amberley Publishing
The Hill, Stroud
Gloucestershire, GL5 4EP

www.amberleybooks.com

Copyright © Mike Hitches & Paul Hughes, 2011

The right of Mike Hitches & Paul Hughes to be identified as the
Authors of this work has been asserted in accordance with the
Copyrights, Designs and Patents Act 1988.

All rights reserved. No part of this book may be reprinted
or reproduced or utilised in any form or by any electronic,
mechanical or other means, now known or hereafter invented,
including photocopying and recording, or in any information
storage or retrieval system, without the permission in writing
from the Publishers.

British Library Cataloguing in Publication Data.
A catalogue record for this book is available from the British Library.

ISBN 978 1 4456 0286 8

Typesetting and Origination by Amberley Publishing.
Printed in Great Britain.

Contents

Introduction	7
The Railways of Whitby	9
Operation and Train Services	23
Motive Power	44
Engine Sheds	53
Evolution of NER Architecture	61
A Walk Around Whitby West Cliff Station	66
End of the Line	114
Sources	127
Acknowledgements	128

A section from the NER tile map at Whitby Town station serves to illustrate Whitby's location within the rail network at the start of the twentieth century. (P. Hughes)

Introduction

Railways arrived early to the Yorkshire fishing town of Whitby. In just thirty years from 1836, they had played a major part in the town's transition from an area heavily dependent on fishing and traditional industries to a busy holiday destination for the newly mobile Victorians. Situated at the crossing point of two railway routes – one along the picturesque coast from industrial Teesside to the growing resort of Scarborough and the other forging inland to connections with the East Coast Main Line at York and routes into the West Riding of Yorkshire – it was ideally situated as a destination for residents of the growing industrial towns to escape for a day in the sea air.

While the principal station was always that on the harbour side, known as Whitby Town, West Cliff station on the coast route served as a busy interchange for travellers between the two lines for almost eighty years. During this time, the West Cliff area of the town was transformed from a greenfield site to a growing, fashionable estate, which quickly filled with hotels and amenities for the town's yearly influx of summer visitors.

Arriving as it did towards the end of the railway-building mania of the mid-nineteenth century, West Cliff station represented the confident approach of a railway that was well established in its business and can be regarded as almost the final development of the North Eastern Railway 'wayside' station.

Despite the hectic services of the summer months, the seasonal imbalance of traffic, operating costs and growing competition from the roads ultimately made the coast route to Middlesbrough an early casualty. It closed long before the sweeping cuts of the mid-1960s. However, the station buildings at West Cliff survived, adapting first to new industrial uses and later becoming housing in the middle of the West Cliff estate, to which they had provided the catalyst for growth almost 140 years earlier.

The Railways of Whitby

West Cliff station at Whitby came into existence in 1883 as part of the Whitby, Redcar & Middlesbrough Union Railway (WR&MUR) and served this growing coastal town as its second station for almost eighty years. The WR&MUR was formed to complete the link from industrial Teesside to Whitby along the Yorkshire coast, from an end-on junction with the Cleveland Railway at Loftus. Royal Assent for the Act of Parliament for the WR&MUR's 15-mile, 3-furlong route, from a proposed junction 93 yards east of Ruswarp on the Whitby to Pickering Railway (W&PR), was received on 16 July 1866. A short branch was also authorised, which would link with the proposed Scarborough & Whitby Railway (S&WR) at Larpool Wood. As we will see, the line as finally completed under the North Eastern Railway differed somewhat from the route originally proposed.

Whitby came onto the railway map at a very early stage, being the first town on the Yorkshire coast to be connected to the new railway network with the opening of the Whitby & Pickering Railway in 1836.

The town had a long tradition of alum working, whaling, shipbuilding and associated maritime servicing industries. However, its isolated location on the Yorkshire coast, with moorland on three sides and the North Sea on the other, had meant that for centuries most of Whitby's trade and communication had come from the sea. In May 1831, local businessmen who were concerned these traditional industries were in decline convened a meeting at the Angel Inn, Whitby, concluding that trade could be enhanced if inland communications were improved. As a result of this meeting, the engineer George Stephenson was asked to survey a railway line inland with trains pulled by horses, which would be simple to construct. His report suggested a line to Pickering would be suitable, which could be used to transport coal and other goods from the port inland to the market towns in the Vale of Ryedale. Agricultural produce and building stone would make the return journey to the coast, for onward shipment by sea.

The Act of Parliament incorporating the Whitby & Pickering Railway was obtained on 6 May 1833 and the contract for the building of the line was let the following August. Work went well, despite the difficult and isolated terrain of the North Yorkshire Moors, through which it passed. A tunnel with castellated portals was built at Grosmont, under Lease Rigg; while at Fen Bog between Goathland and Newton Dale, Stephenson solved problems with laying the track over the unstable ground, by laying a foundation of heather bound in sheepskins and hurdles covered in moss. All of this came at a price, the total cost of construction being £105,000, which was more than double the original estimate for the 24-mile route. During the line's construction, iron stone deposits were found in the Grosmont and Beck Hole areas, bringing a new and unanticipated source of traffic for the railway.

When the railway opened, trains were horse-drawn from Whitby to Beck Hole, south of Grosmont, then rope-hauled up a 1 in 14 incline, taking around 5 minutes to ascend. Once over the summit, gravity took the trains through Newton Dale at speeds of up to 30 miles an hour, before being horse-hauled for the final 4 miles to Pickering.

In 1845, the Whitby & Pickering became part of the 'Railway King' George Hudson's York & North Midland Railway (Y&NMR) empire, largely due to financial difficulties from the high construction costs forcing its sale. Although the W&PR was successful, the directors were aware that they needed investment from a larger company. By the end of 1836 they were in debt to the tune of £13,000, leading to an Act being obtained in 1837 to raise an extra £30,000 of capital. It was also becoming apparent that the shipment of iron ore from Grosmont to Whitby was uneconomical, taking ten men and twenty horses to transport just 120 tons of iron stone. All of this served to highlight the need to upgrade the line if it was to remain viable.

While a merger with the Stockton & Darlington Railway (S&D) was considered, it was Hudsons' Y&NMR that eventually assumed control of the W&PR, giving connections to West Yorkshire and eventually industrial Lancashire. It is interesting to speculate on how Britain's railway map may have been altered had the W&PR merged with the S&D at this time. The York & North Midland wasted little time in connecting their new asset to their York to Scarborough route, with a 7-mile extension from Pickering. This was commenced in 1845, at a cost of £80,000, crossing flat terrain to end with a junction facing to eastbound trains at Rillington, close to the market town of Malton. George Hudson envisaged that, through the purchase of the W&PR, Whitby could be developed for tourism, and embarked on an ambitious development in the West Cliff area of the town, known as Cliff Fields at that time.

This idea had first been considered by Whitby businessmen as long ago as 1827, but other than forming a Joint Stock Committee, little progress had been made. Hudson first came to Whitby in 1843 at the height of his railway speculation, to set up the Whitby Building Company. However, other business commitments had meant it was 1848 before the Whitby Building Company came to buy the whole of the West Cliff estate. Construction started immediately, with the first buildings to appear being the Royal Hotel and the imposing East Crescent. The official architect for the project was John Dobson, who was responsible for Newcastle Central railway station. Boarding houses followed the Royal Hotel, as originally proposed in 1827 under the Joint Stock Committee's plans for the town. Langdale Terrace at one end and Belle Vue Terrace at the other bookended four adjoining streets: John Street, Normanby Terrace, Abbey Terrace and Hudson Street – carrying the name of its innovator.

As the crowning glory of this development, Hudson had planned a magnificent seaward-facing crescent to rival that of Bath. However, before this could be finished, his tightly stretched finances snapped. He owed money to lenders, who had continued to advance him sums without ensuring he had the ability to repay. Hudson's railway empire was not providing the returns at first envisaged and he had used the West Cliff estate as security on his loans. So it was in 1849 that George Hudson was declared bankrupt. The grand East Crescent was never completed and stands to this day only half finished. However, despite its inauspicious end, Hudson's Whitby Building Company provided a strong foundation for what was to follow.

Once linked to the Y&NMR, Hudson set about the rebuilding of the W&PR to heavier standards, to allow locomotive haulage. This involved doubling the track and replacing bridges with stronger, wider structures, as well as building new stations at Whitby and Pickering. A new Deviation Line was built to avoid the troublesome Beck Hole incline and included a new station at Goathland. The conversion to allow locomotive haulage took place in two stages, with the Pickering to Levisham section opening on 1 September 1845. This was originally worked as a single line, the second running line coming into use a year later, following inspection by Captain Coddington on behalf of Her Majesty's Railway Inspectorate. The same report questioned workmanship on the Levisham to Goathland section, delaying its opening until 8 June 1847. The wooden sleepers and rail fixings used in this work were brought to Whitby by ship, imported from the Baltic.

Whitby eventually achieved its link to the industrial North East – by a roundabout route – in 1865, with the completion of a line from Grosmont to Picton along the Esk Valley. A more direct line to Middlesbrough was achieved in 1868, with a short branch from Battersby to Nunthorpe, bypassing Eaglescliffe and linking with the S&D's 1853 Middlesbrough to Guisborough line. At this time, the Cleveland Railway were pushing south down the coast to Loftus (formerly Lofthouse), where the coastal link to Whitby would be completed when the WR&MUR arrived in 1883.

The NER took control of the S&D in 1863, although this company retained much of its independence for many years as the Central Division of the NER. As a result of a threat to their monopoly, the West Hartlepool Harbour & Railway Company and the Cleveland Railway were taken over by the NER in 1865. This resulted in the NER completing the Cleveland Railway's Loftus branch, which was opened on 27 May 1867. The through route along the cost to Whitby would be completed by the WR&MUR at a time when growing leisure travel and seaside tourism, along with Hudson's bold development on the West Cliff, saw Whitby expand rapidly. The vision of the Whitby businessmen of 1831, who instigated the building of the W&PR in the hope that by improving inland transport links their town could flourish, were being realised.

The Whitby, Redcar & Middlesbrough Union Railway was a poorly funded and weakly engineered project from the start. Work finally commenced on 3 May 1871, when the Dowager Marchioness of Normanby cut the first sod at Sandsend. The WR&MUR had an authorised capital of £250,000 in £10 shares, with permission to borrow a further £83,000. The directors were the Marquis of Normanby – of Mulgrave Castle and principal landowner in the area – who was chairman, along with industrialist Charles Palmer of Palmer's iron and steel works and ship yard at Jarrow. The Palmer Company was mining iron stone at that time at Port Mulgrave near Staithes on the intended route of the line, which Palmer was currently sending to Jarrow by sea. The final director was John Henry Dillon, of Albany, London.

A year after work begun, the proposed connection with the NER at Whitby was altered from the junction at Larpool – facing to Down (Whitby-bound) trains – to one at Bog Hall, much nearer Whitby Town station – facing to Up trains. This shortened the line to 16 miles 23 chains and provided a connection at Whitby, which was better from a civil engineer's point of view, but perhaps ultimately less so operationally. The proposed connection with the Scarborough & Whitby line was dropped, but this would later be achieved by the S&WR themselves, joining the WR&MUR at Airy Hill (later known as Prospect Hill Junction) on West Cliff, before the WR&MUR began its descent to the riverside connection with the W&PR at Bog Hall.

Work on the line was slow and the directors were unhappy with the contractor, Dicksons, which appears to suggest they were unable to finance the project. As a safeguard, the WR&MUR decided in September 1873 that two of the contractor's locomotives would stand as security, to a value of £2,000. They insisted a plate be fixed to these locos, displaying their ownership by the WR&MUR, in the event that the contractor should go into liquidation. Only three months later, Dicksons lost the contract and all of the plant and materials were duly taken over by the railway company.

In May 1874, the WR&MUR decided to sell off the equipment obtained from the contractor and had the two locos – *Penwyllt* and *Mulgrave* – valued by Morrisons of London. It was estimated that due to its poor state of repair, *Penwyllt* was worth only £775 and *Mulgrave* £875, as this machine had done little work. The locos were duly put up for sale, *Mulgrave* going to T. B. Nelson of York for £750 and *Penwyllt* to Morrison, the valuer, for £600. The contractor's horses were sold for £471 17s 2d.

On 1 July 1875, the NER leased the WR&MUR in perpetuity at a minimum rental of £4,500 per annum, with the option of taking full control after it had been open for ten years. The NER was to receive half of the gross receipts to set against the cost of working the line, along with 4½ per cent on the capital raised to finish construction. This was all ratified by the WR&MUR Act of 19 July 1875. The NER undertook all liabilities to complete the line in a 'substantial and

Whitby West Cliff Station

The northern portal of the 308-yard-long Kettleness tunnel during the LNER days. The portal – now bricked up – can by seen today from the Cleveland Way. (R. S. Carpenter/M. Hitches collection)

satisfactory manner', accepting a tender from John Waddell & Son of Edinburgh to carry out the necessary works at a price of £145,666 2s, later amended to £146,163 12s. The agreed completion date of 13 July 1881 was not met.

The line proved difficult to build due to the coastal terrain it traversed, with a number of deep valleys at right angles to the sea to be crossed. These difficulties were compounded by the poor work of the previous contractor, much of which had to be repeated. During the time that construction had been suspended, part of the formation had fallen into the sea, leading to a new route being followed that required two substantial tunnels to be built: at Sandsend of 1 mile 652 yards in length, and at Kettleness, of 308 yards. The northern end of Sandsend tunnel ran close to the cliff face, allowing a short service gallery to be dug to the cliff side to enable the contractor to dump spoil in the sea. The five steel viaducts over the deep valleys were a constant source of concern for the WR&MUR throughout its working life and ultimately contributed to its early closure. Poor work from the original contractor delayed completion, while rapid corrosion in the salt air lead to frequent heavy repairs during their working lives. It was not until 3 December 1883, almost two and a half years late, that the first train to Saltburn left Whitby Town station.

No formal celebrations accompanied its departure that Monday morning, but a large number of local people gathered at Whitby Town station well before the time of departure, hoping to obtain tickets for the various stations on the route. Such was the demand that extra carriages had to be added and many passengers travelled without tickets. Despite this, on the first day some 479 tickets were issued at Whitby Town, with a further 352 at West Cliff. The intermediate stations were decorated with flags, with many turning out along the line to cheer the inaugural train. The local newspaper of the time cheerfully reported that the first day went without a hitch, despite some late running, which it seems was not out of the ordinary even then. It goes on to commend the ride as 'the smoothest and easiest they had ever travelled on', describing the station at West Cliff as being 'soundly built' and 'erected especially for the residents and visitors in that fashionable locality'. By this time the West Cliff area was growing rapidly. Despite Hudson's collapse, the West Cliff estate had been purchased by colliery owner George Elliot, who saw this new area of the town strive towards its full potential as a resort, much as Hudson had envisaged.

The railway line along the coast was popular with tourists from the start, thanks to its seaside views, reputed to be among the best in the country. It was also famous for the five graceful, tubular steel viaducts across the valleys. Travelling north, the first of these to be encountered was at Upgang, three quarters of a mile from West Cliff station. It was 330 feet long and 70 feet high, with five 60-foot spans and one of 27 feet 6 inches. Its close proximity to the sea meant it required extensive repairs as early as 1893/94, as salt corrosion had undermined the integrity of its trusses. Next was Newholm Beck, a viaduct of 330 feet in length, with nine 30-foot spans and two 57-foot 6-inch spans, at a height of 50 feet. This location was popular with photographers and

A classic WR&MUR view, 80116 crossing Sandsend Beck with the sea behind. The route hugged the coast for most of its length, giving spectacular views. (D. Blackwell collection)

features in many pictures of the line, due to its proximity to the Whitby to Sandsend road.

East Row viaduct at Sandsend was the lowest of these structures at only 30 feet above the valley floor and was so close to the coast that the sea went beneath it at high tide. It was 528 feet long with five 60-foot spans and two of 28 feet 9 inches. In 1905, even greater repairs were needed here than had been required at Upgang ten years earlier. The salt-laden atmosphere had destroyed the trusses, which were replaced completely with prefabricated steel ones. Immediately south of Sandsend station was Sandsend viaduct, with the station platform running up to the start of its deck. It had two stone arches over a road at the southern end and five steel spans of varying lengths over the valley.

The final viaduct was by far the most spectacular, at 730 feet in length and a maximum height of 152 feet, adjacent to Staithes station. This considerable structure consisted of six 60-foot spans and eleven of 30 feet. Following the Tay Bridge disaster in July 1881, the NER were advised that they should strengthen this structure, adding two additional rows of bracing and wheel guards to prevent trains from being blown over in strong winds. An anemometer was attached to the viaduct to measure wind speed. This device rang a bell in Staithes signal box, alerting the signalman not to allow trains to pass over the viaduct if conditions were too windy. Trains from the north were authorised to be propelled back to Grinkle under these circumstances if necessary.

All of these viaducts were demolished during 1960 following the closure of the WR&MUR, but the footings of the Sandsend viaducts are still visible today. The steel tubes that formed the viaduct legs were cut up on site, leaving large cylinders of concrete from their cores, which were reused in coastal defence work and are still evident, protecting the bays which they once spanned from erosion.

The final part of the railway along the Yorkshire coast was provided with the opening of the Scarborough & Whitby Railway in 1885. This route not only linked the two coastal resort towns, but finally allowed through running from Middlesbrough to Scarborough, bringing tourists in the summer months and providing a vital link for the communities it served during the harsh winters.

The line between Whitby and Scarborough had its origins in an Act of July 1865, but insufficient capital was raised, resulting in no further progress being made until 1870, when a proposition was made to construct an isolated line from Gallows Close in Scarborough to Gideon's Timber Pond on the east side of the River Esk at Whitby. Royal Assent was granted on 29 June 1871 and the Scarborough & Whitby Railway Company was authorised to raise capital of £120,000. Work was started near Scarborough cemetery on 3 June 1872 by the contractor Kirk & Parry, under the guidance of the project engineer Eugenius Birch, who was to become famous as a Victorian pier builder.

The first 7 miles from Scarborough were ready for ballast and track laying by August the next year, by which time an Act had been obtained authorising a junction with the NER at Falsgrave, Scarborough, and with the WR&MUR at Prospect Hill, Whitby. To achieve these junctions, a curved 183-yard-long tunnel was required at Scarborough and to cross the Esk to the graceful Larpool viaduct at Whitby. This was the biggest civil engineering work on the route. However, building was slow and by 1877 had stopped altogether due to lack of funds. At this time, there were calls from a group of shareholders for the receivers to be brought in to wind the company up.

Whitby West Cliff Station

A southbound Class A8 crossing Newholm Beck viaduct in the 1950s. (D. Blackwell collection)

The largest of the viaducts was at Staithes. The original build specification called for the tubular steel uprights to be filled with concrete, but during inspections in the 1930s all the viaducts were found to be filled with gravel. This forced the LNER to design a special machine to inject concrete into the uprights under pressure. The high maintenance costs of the viaducts contributed to the early closure of the WR&MUR. (R. S. Carpenter/ M. Hitches collection)

The Railways of Whitby

Larpool viaduct carried the S&WR across the valley of the River Esk at Whitby. This present-day view was taken from the trackbed of the WR&MUR, curving up from Bog Hall, with the W&PR following the riverbank below. (P. Hughes)

Prospect Hill Junction, Whitby. The WR&MUR is in the centre, passing under the signal box to join with the S&WR, which runs under the right arch of the bridge. (D. Blackwell collection)

Whitby West Cliff Station

The unusual overhead signal box at Prospect Hill Junction. This view is towards West Cliff, taken from a northbound train on the S&WR. The WR&MUR is on the left. (A. Brown)

The Railways of Whitby

Above and below: Railway posters promoting the resort of Whitby. (M. Hitches collection)

Whitby West Cliff Station

New efforts were made to complete the project in 1879, resulting in an Act being passed on 12 August 1880 reviving powers for completion of the railway and authorising further capital to be raised. Sir Charles Fox & Son of Westminster were appointed as the new engineers of the line, while the building contract was let to John Waddell & Son, who had completed the WR&MUR. Work restarted in 1881, with the line finally opening to regular traffic on 16 July 1885. Due to difficulties associated with the construction, the cost had spiralled from the original estimate of £157,000 to £649,813. As can be seen, none of the railways serving Whitby were completed within their original estimated costs.

The official opening of the S&WR took place a day before public services commenced, on 15 July 1885, with a special train for the directors of the company and dignitaries from Whitby and Scarborough. The train was provided by the NER, who operated the line as part of their own network from the outset. As with the opening train of the WR&MUR, this director's special left Scarborough with no ceremony, but was cheered on route by workmen and well-wishers. Making brief stops at the eight intermediate stations, the train took an hour and ten minutes to complete its journey, arriving at West Cliff at 12.45. Lunch was provided at Whitby's Crown Hotel before returning at 13.45. The non-stop return trip took just under an hour, a journey time that would remain typical throughout the working lifetime of the line. The directors and around two hundred guests completed their day out by banqueting at the Royal Hotel, Scarborough. On the first day of public services, extra trains had to be provided to meet the demand. Most passengers chose to travel to Robin Hood's Bay from the respective ends and return, rather than make the full journey.

Operation and Train Services

The Saltburn to Whitby line was of double track for most of its length, but at Loftus, at the commencement of the WR&MUR, the line became single with passing places at Grinkle, Staithes, Hinderwell and West Cliff. Later an additional platform and loop was also provided at Kettleness, but Sandsend never had a passing loop at all. When the S&WR opened in 1885, this too was comprised of a single running line, with passing areas at some stations.

In the early years, these stretches of single line were controlled by the 'Train Staff and Ticket' method, to ensure only one train was ever on a single-line section between passing areas. The principle involved the provision of a unique 'Train Staff' for each single-line section, which must be carried by the driver of each train to pass over that section and be given up to the signalman at the end. In the event that successive trains needed to travel through a section before one returned in the opposite direction to return the staff, a written ticket was issued to the driver of the first train, who was shown the staff but not allowed to carry it. The staff would be carried by the final train to travel the section in the same direction, thus leaving it at the correct end for the next planned movement. The signalmen at opposite ends of the single line sections communicated with each other using a telegraph-based bell code system, which was adopted nationwide – a derived version of which remains in use to this day.

While the Staff and Ticket system was simple, it only worked well if traffic patterns were regular and predictable. Problems arose if additional or unexpected trains needed to be run at short notice, when it might be found that the staff was at the opposite end of the section to the train that needed to depart. Through the early twentieth century, Staff and Ticket working was replaced widely by Electric Token Block.

Whitby West Cliff Station

Tyer's No. 6 tablet machines, like this one at Grosmont on the North Yorkshire Moors railway, were used on all the single lines in the Whitby area. The tokens were stored in the lower part of the machine, and dispensed into the drawer at the bottom. The curved upper part displayed when tokens were withdrawn for Up or Down trains. This particular machine was originally used at Hinderwell. (P. Hughes)

Operation and Train Services

This involved a similar principle, in that the driver of each train on a single-line section carried an object of authority to proceed – in this case the token. It differed in that multiple tokens existed for each section, stored securely in electrically interlocked machines, which were designed to allow only one token to be available for use at any one time. In addition, the token could not be removed from the holding machine without the signalman at the opposite end of the single-line section electrically releasing it. Once a token had been dispensed, no others could be withdrawn from either machine until the first had either been taken through the section and placed into the machine at the other end, or restored to the machine from which it was obtained. As a further security measure in later years, the levers operating signals controlling entry onto a single line were electrically locked until the token had been dispensed from the relevant machine.

Staff and Ticket working was finally banned from use on passenger railways on 31 January 1931, by which time the LNER had replaced it with more modern methods of working. The Electric Token system was widely adopted for single-line working nationwide, with a variety of different designs of token machines in use. The NER and, in later years, the LNER favoured the equipment from the London manufacturer Tyer & Company. Hence, Tyer's No. 6 token instruments were in use across the NER and exclusively in the Whitby area. As the level of services in the summer months rose through the LNER period, the single-line sections proved to be the factor limiting train frequency on the Saltburn to Scarborough route.

When the WR&MUR was opened under the NER in 1883, the service was operated between Whitby Town and Saltburn but, following the opening of the through route to Scarborough just over a year later, most trains ran from Scarborough to Saltburn and return. This left the connection to the Town station being provided by a shuttle service. By 1910, this had changed to six Whitby Town to Saltburn trains in each direction and five Whitby Town to Scarborough trains, connecting with each other at West Cliff. This will have removed the need for the shuttle services, which from an operational point of view, were a time-consuming exercise for such a short run, requiring as it did the train to be run round in the Middlesbrough-bound platform at West Cliff, then propelled out onto the single line to the north, ready to depart again to Town from the Scarborough-bound platform. This was because the Middlesbrough-bound Up platform was not signalled for bi-directional

Whitby West Cliff Station

British Railways Standard Class 4 2-6-4Ts worked many of the local services in the final years of operation. Here we see 80118 in a classic West Cliff view, with the Co-op Creamery in the background and the distinctive footbridge, along with a lovely NER slotted post signal and water tank. (D. Blackwell collection)

A Middlesbrough-bound Class A6 on a sunny 1950s afternoon. (N. Cholmondeley collection)

Operation and Train Services

Timetable from the 1922 Bradshaw. (M. Hitches collection)

working and facing point locks were not provided in the Scarborough-bound direction from this platform. The same time-consuming run round will have also been needed at Whitby Town station.

Generally in this country, northbound trains are referred to as travelling in the Down direction, with Up trains travelling south. However, this was not the case on the WR&MUR, as Middlesbrough-bound trains, which travelled in a northerly direction for most of their journey, were referred to as Up, with those from Saltburn being regarded as travelling in the Down direction. This curious reversal of the normal

Whitby West Cliff Station

A Malton-bound Ivatt tank crossing the junction with the WR&MUR at Bog Hall on the banks of the River Esk. (D. Blackwell collection)

rule was probably as a result of the nature of the WR&MUR's junction with the NER at Bog Hall. Trains leaving Whitby Town departed in the Up direction, as the bias of the W&PR, towards Malton and York, was southerly. But in the case of those taking the junction for the WR&MUR, that bias quickly shifted to predominantly northbound and continued as such all the way to Saltburn and Middlesbrough. The NER would often change the directional terminology after such junctions, but for some reason this was not done in the case of the coast route, which continued north in the Up direction all the way to Middlesbrough and onwards to Northallerton, where it joined the southbound East Coast Main Line.

During the NER period, a number of short workings on the S&WR were introduced between Scarborough and Cloughton, four times a

Operation and Train Services

day, which, by the grouping, had been extended to Staintondale and had been supplemented on the WR&MUR section by two Whitby Town–Hinderwell trains. These were typically operated by autocars and later by Sentinel steam railcars – an early forerunner of the multiple unit stock with which we are familiar today. The departures from Saltburn remained largely unaltered during this period. These short workings continued into the LNER period for a further ten years, but by the summer of 1932 they had been discontinued, leaving six Saltburn and six Scarborough departures.

The first alteration to the signalling arrangements at West Cliff was made to facilitate the reversal in the Middlesbrough-bound platform of the Scarborough trains around 1910. It involved the provision of a facing point lock and a starting signal for southbound trains in the Middlesbrough platform. It was a requirement under Board of Trade regulations that all facing points over which a passenger train was to run must be fitted with a locking device. The provision of this equipment at the south end will have removed the need for the set to be propelled out and drawn back into the Scarborough platform to depart. It is likely that the calling on arm under the Down Home signal, allowing locos to enter the occupied platform to run round, was provided as new with the frame, as its number fits within the original sequence, unlike later alterations.

The early 1930s saw the coastal lines becoming increasingly busy during the summer months, leading the LNER to make considerable improvements along the whole route to improve line capacity and infrastructure. From the start of the 1933 summer timetable, the northern terminus was changed from Saltburn to Middlesbrough. Initially, all trains from Middlesbrough travelled via Nunthorpe and Guisborough, but in later summers some were routed through Redcar as well. Five through trains from Middlesbrough to Scarborough were provided, with two Middlesbrough to Whitby returns in the evening to collect homeward-bound day trippers. Extra trains frequently had to be run to keep pace with demand, leading to the 1934 timetable being increased to nine through trains a day.

With the introduction of the Middlesbrough to Scarborough service, the need for a connecting shuttle to Whitby Town returned. To accommodate this, the loading dock at the south end of West Cliff's Scarborough-bound platform was lengthened in 1934, with a wooden extension to provide a short passenger bay long enough to hold two

Whitby West Cliff Station

The bay platform is visible on the right in this picture, which was taken just after closure. A wooden extension had increased the length to two coaches. (N. Cholmondeley collection)

coaches. A new facing connection was provided to allow trains from Town station to run directly into this. It had been suggested that the Middlesbrough-bound platform could be converted into an island, at an estimated cost of £3,183, to handle this traffic, but the bay was seen as a cheaper alternative. The shuttle trains consisted of one, or later two, Sentinel railcars, which alleviated the need to run round at each end.

Further increases to the number of trains were made over the following summers, peaking in 1938 with twelve through trains, as well as excursion and freight traffic. Consideration was given to providing passing loops at Hawsker and Fyling Hall on the S&WR section, and Sandsend on the WR&MUR, to increase line capacity further, but the problem was that the summer timetable only operated for ten weeks and the railway ran far below capacity for the rest of the year. These

Operation and Train Services

alterations might have taken place, if it had not been for the beginning of the Second World War. The summer of 1939 saw fewer travellers than the previous year, with the uncertainty of what lay ahead leading to many people choosing to stay at home that summer.

During the summer timetables in the mid-1930s, goods trains were generally run in the early hours to leave the single-line sections clear for passenger traffic through the day. The pick up goods trains were worked from the Whitby end of the WR&MUR, going as far as Carlin How on the Saltburn line. They would leave Town station at 03.45, taking refuge on the double track north of Loftus, before returning to Whitby in time for the first passenger departure of the day at 06.45. The S&WR section was subject to similar limitations, with the goods train leaving Scarborough Goods Yard, Gallows Close, at 23.45, arriving at Whitby at 00.50, before making the return journey and shunting through the early hours. In the winter months, both goods trains ran during the day.

After the war, intensive summer services were gradually restored, peaking in 1954 at fourteen departures daily, most of which were through trains from Middlesbrough to Scarborough. Some ran via Redcar, with around 2½ hours for the 58-mile journey being a typical

An unusual view of a Class J28 crossing Upgang viaduct with a short freight train, probably in the 1920s. Note the lettering on the wagons. (R. S. Carpenter/M. Hitches collection)

time. Slightly fewer trains ran on Sundays, with six trains leaving Middlesbrough in the morning and returning from Scarborough through the early evening, at half-hourly intervals. By this time the Sentinel railcars had been withdrawn, so the shuttle to Town station was provided by loco-hauled two-coach sets. To alleviate the need for the time-consuming and capacity-blocking run rounds at each end, special dispensation was granted, allowing these trains to be propelled from Whitby Town to West Cliff. Propelling of passenger trains was not normally allowed under the operating rules and regulations. This short trip from Whitby Town to West Cliff involved climbing the steep curve from Bog Hall to Prospect Hill on a rising 1 in 54, so by insisting the propelling loco always remained at the Town end, any danger of a runaway was prevented.

During the most intensely operated periods, the pick-up goods train, which ran on Tuesdays, Thursdays and Saturdays by this time, again had to fit around the passenger service without causing delay. Summer Saturdays were so busy that the goods were not run at all, but unlike the pre-war summer services, it was not necessary to time these trains through the night. The train was always worked from the Whitby end, going north in the morning and returning in mid-afternoon. However, the winter passenger service was reduced to just four trains each way and the goods three times a week, with no shuttles and no weekend service at all.

By the late 1950s, this seasonal imbalance was starting to take its toll. The regular all year round service was being hit hard by competition from the roads, and in 1958 British Railways blamed the high operating and maintenance costs of the WR&MUR – principally that of the viaducts and anticipated repairs to stabilise Sandsend tunnel – as the reason for their decision to close the line from West Cliff to Loftus. Unlike later closures in the mid-1960s, the decision went largely unopposed and the last train on the WR&MUR from Middlesbrough to Scarborough ran on 3 May 1958, hauled by Standard Class 4 2-6-4T 80116. It was greeted by small groups of well wishers on its way, carrying a headboard with the title 'The Economist'. From the following Monday, 5 May, an enhanced service was provided on the remaining lines serving Whitby, using new DMU sets. The new diesel trains were only slightly faster than their predecessors, but were quicker to make the reversals at West Cliff, Town and Scarborough, as well as Battersby on the Esk Valley line. On routes better known for their scenery than

Operation and Train Services

Trains crossing at West Cliff in the 1950s. (H. B. Priestley/M. Hitches collection)

speed, the new units offered passengers improved views, while their open-plan seating allowed tickets to be sold on the trains, leading to the removal of staff from some of the smaller stations. A majority of the trains on the Whitby to Malton line became DMU operated in April 1959, leading to the engine sheds at Whitby Town and Pickering closing at this time.

Following the closure of the WR&MUR in 1958, the line was cut at West Cliff, with buffers installed near the Upgang Lane road bridge, north of the station. Track and equipment was recovered from the Middlesbrough end, with the route being cleared over the next two years. West Cliff stayed open for another three years after this as the terminus of the line from Scarborough and kept its goods facilities, served as required by the Malton pick-up. West Cliff handled all the coal traffic for Whitby, as no depots were provided at the town station.

Whitby West Cliff Station

A Class L1 heading south off Staithes viaduct in 1958. (R. S. Carpenter/M. Hitches collection)

Standard Class 4 tank 80117, a Whitby loco, setting back onto its train at West Cliff, having run round the coaches. These reversals were a common operational feature throughout the working life of the station. (N. Cholmondeley collection)

Operation and Train Services

Upgang viaduct with Whitby visible in the background. Class L1 67764 is heading northward with a Scarborough to Middlesbrough train. (R. S. Carpenter/M. Hitches collection)

Standard Class 4 tank 80116 heading north at Staithes. The additional handrails on the viaduct were to prevent passengers stepping from the front coaches of trains that had drawn beyond the platform end and falling from the viaduct! (D. Blackwell collection)

Whitby West Cliff Station

The scale of Staithes viaduct is evident in this view. (D. Blackwell collection)

A Class L1 skirts a headland despoiled by alum working, north of Sandsend in 1958. Sandsend station and viaduct are visible in the left background. (R. S. Carpenter/M. Hitches collection)

Operation and Train Services

A J25 fitted with a snow plough shunting wagons at Whitby shed in July 1956. (M. Hitches collection)

Class G5 1889 stands in the sunshine at Whitby Town station in June 1934. Note the tail lamp on the back of the engine. Hopefully the driver removed this before departure; otherwise the signalman at Whitby will have had to send the 'stop and examine train' signal to his counterpart at Bog Hall. (R. S. Carpenter/M. Hitches collection)

Whitby West Cliff Station

A passenger train on the WR&MUR approaching Staithes in the early twentieth century. Staithes was the only WR&MUR station on which the signal box was not situated on the same platform as the main building. Its location on the opposite platform, just visible to the left, gave the signalman better views of trains arriving from the south due to the curving approach. The station staff in this picture appear to be posing for the photographer. (Lens of Sutton/M. Hitches collection)

Whitby shed's 80116 draws a short train into Sandsend station, just a month before the WR&MUR's closure in 1958. (R. S. Carpenter/M. Hitches collection)

Operation and Train Services

This Standard Class 3 2-6-0 is leaving West Cliff for Scarborough. The 'class one' head code indicates the train will not stop at all intermediate stations. (N. Cholmondeley collection)

A Class V1 2-6-2T in the 1950s. Signalling alterations must have been taking place at this time; note the ground signal on the platform near the signal box. (N. Cholmondeley collection)

Whitby West Cliff Station

The pick-up goods in the hands of a J21, probably in the early 1920s. (J. Alsop collection)

A Class J72 loco shunting in Scarborough Goods Yard at Gallows Close. (D. Blackwell collection)

Operation and Train Services

Another A8, with 'class one' head codes, on a special train in 1957. Note the RCTS headboard and 'main line' coaching stock. The set is 'topped and tailed', with a second loco at the rear. The A8 appears to be in the process of coupling onto the set; note the fireman on the track, while the driver watches on. (N. Cholmondeley collection)

The exposed location of Staithes viaduct is evident in this view of a departing northbound train in April 1958, just a few days before closure. An anemometer on the viaduct warned the signalman if the wind was too strong for trains to cross. It is just visible, between the loco and the home signal in the centre of the picture. (R. S. Carpenter/M. Hitches collection)

Whitby West Cliff Station

Running round of sets in the Middlesbrough-bound platform was a daily occurrence at West Cliff prior to the closure of the WR&MUR in 1958 and the introduction of DMU sets in the final years of the station's operational life. (A. Brown collection)

When this picture of Class A6 693 was taken in June 1935, the coast route was approaching its busiest time before the Second World War. The destination board on the side of the brake coach reads 'Scarborough'. (P. Hughes collection)

This may well have influenced the decision to keep the station open after the rest of the WR&MUR was closed. A frequent perk on the NER and LNER stations was that of allowing the stationmaster to trade as a coal merchant, using railway property as his base. There were conditions attached to this privilege, including allowing the railway auditors to inspect his books, but he was allowed to keep all the profits. At some stations this could be greater than his salary as stationmaster.

West Cliff station was finally closed on 10 May 1961, at the start of the summer timetable. The track was further cut back to just north of Prospect Hill Junction, leaving a short spur, long enough to allow the Scarborough trains to change direction. By this time, a majority of services on the Scarborough line were DMU operated; loco-hauled sets were topped and tailed between Whitby Town and Prospect Hill, to avoid the need to run round here. A set of stop blocks was installed at the end of the spur, but the track as far as West Cliff remained *in situ* until around 1963, and was occasionally used by engineers' trains recovering material from the West Cliff site.

The Scarborough line itself closed on 6 March 1965, with the last of the track in the Whitby area removed by 1973. A majority of the track on the S&WR route had been removed during 1968, but the possibility of a pot ash mine being sunk at Hawsker, south of Whitby, lead to British Railways leaving the track *in situ* from here to Prospect Hill Junction and the last stub of the WR&MUR down to Bog Hall, with minimal signalling retained. This was to facilitate the removal of the pot ash to Middlesbrough via Prospect Hill and the Esk Valley line. Ultimately, the mine was established at Boulby, between Loftus and Staithes, on the section of the WR&MUR closed in 1958. This led to part of the route being relayed on the original trackbed from Loftus to the new mine. This is now the only part of the former WR&MUR in use. The overhead signal box at Prospect Hill burned down around 1971, but the remains of this structure and the substantial civil engineering around the junction are still evident. The trackbed to Scarborough is now a footpath.

Motive Power

At the turn of the century, passenger trains on the WR&MUR were in the hands of T. W. Worsdell and Wilson-Worsdell engines of the NER, including Class A 2-4-2Ts and Class O 0-4-4Ts, with goods traffic handled by Class P and P1 0-6-0s. Prior to the introduction of the NER class D 4-4-4Ts, several loco types appeared in the Whitby area. In these early years, 2-4-0 and 0-6-0 types were used on summer excursions, with BTP 0-4-4Ts and McDonnell 0-6-0s on the Saltburn to Whitby trains, with lighter 0-6-0s handling goods traffic.

In 1905, the NER introduced the autocar service between Whitby and Kettleness to Sleights along the Esk Valley and to Robin Hood's Bay on the S&WR, using a BTP 0-4-4T and a single coach with a driving compartment in the rear. Under the LNER, six-cylinder Sentinel railcars were operated on the West Cliff to Town shuttles and the short workings.

The LNER expressed interest in these vehicles following the Sentinel Company's display at the 1924 British Empire Exhibition, and trialled one of their machines extensively the same year. Two cars were purchased for use in East Anglia, but it was not until 1927 that railcars were introduced into the north-eastern area. However, over the next year, a total of twenty-two vehicles were bought from Sentinel for use on these lines. During the 1930s, three railcars were regularly based at Whitby. One would work all day on the Shuttle service and, on Tuesdays and Fridays, would work an additional late trip, arriving at Scarborough at 22.15. This was to collect passengers who had visited the open-air theatre, whose productions finished at around 22.30. It would return to Whitby via the S&WR and West Cliff in the early hours, reaching the Town station at 00.15. Another Sentinel was deployed on Glaisdale and Goathland short workings, while the final

Motive Power

A Sentinel railcar in the Bay Platform at Whitby Town. (R. S. Carpenter/M. Hitches collection)

vehicle made a lengthy afternoon journey all the way to Ferryhill, via Battersby, Picton and Stockton. As summer traffic became heavier, one railcar proved inadequate on the West Cliff shuttles, so permission was granted in 1935 for these cars to be used in pairs. For technical reasons, they had to be coupled with their boiler compartments outermost.

During the quieter winter months, two Sentinels were sufficient for the Whitby services, one working on Scarborough–Middlesbrough turns via West Cliff and Town and the other on the Shuttle and afternoon Ferryhill service.

In 1907, the NER introduced Class W 4-6-0Ts, with No. 690 based at Saltburn for the Scarborough trains. These engines were rebuilt in later years as 4-6-2Ts, to become the LNER class A6, the famous 'Whitby Tanks', which operated the Middlesbrough–Saltburn–Whitby–Scarborough trains alongside the equally successful A8s for many years.

45

Whitby West Cliff Station

LNER Class H1 (former NER Class D) 4-4-4s were used extensively on the coast services. (D. Blackwell collection)

The A8 4-6-2Ts were perhaps the best-known class of locomotives to operate on the WR&MUR. They were, in fact, rebuilds of an earlier Raven design of 4-4-4 tank engine, the NER class D first introduced in 1913. They were designed to be as easy running bunker-first as chimney-first and were the largest of their time, with an 8-foot firebox with a grate area of 23 square feet, heating an 11-foot-long boiler of 4-foot 9-inch diameter. With a Schmidt superheater, they had a heating area of 1,253 square feet. Boiler pressure was 175 psi, feeding three cylinders with Stephenson link valve gear.

Originally thirty of these locomotives were ordered from Darlington Works, but only twenty were ultimately delivered, due to the start of the First World War. Although used widely across the North East, their most difficult route was Saltburn–Whitby–Scarborough. Unfortunately,

Motive Power

The LNER Class A6 were known as 'Whitby Tanks'. Here, 693 poses under West Cliff's footbridge in June 1935. Note the shuttle set in the Bay platform on the right. (P. Hughes collection)

the steep gradients and sharp curves, especially around Ravenscar and Robin Hood's Bay on the S&WR and Sandsend on the WR&MUR, proved unsuitable for these 4-4-4s. However, the Class Ds were quick and free running in good conditions, but were inclined to slip on greasy rails, needing careful handling under the conditions frequently encountered on the coast route. They were reclassified H1 at the time of the grouping.

In the early LNER period, the former NER branch lines needed further large tank engines, leading to the new CME Nigel Gresley opting to have thirteen ex-Great Central Railway 9N 4-6-2Ts built for the North East coastal routes. So successful were these engines, that in 1928, seven were sent to Saltburn to replace aging H1s on the

Whitby West Cliff Station

A Class A8 4-6-2 approaching Prospect Hill Junction from Scarborough. Rebuilt from the H1s in the 1930s, these locos proved ideal for the Whitby routes. (N. Cholmondeley collection)

Ex-NER Class J25 0-6-0s were used on freight workings throughout the NER, LNER and BR periods. 65700 is seen here shunting at Bog Hall. (Lens of Sutton/M. Hitches collection)

Motive Power

A pleasing study of a Class G5 tank, standing outside Whitby Town's train shed. The loco appears to have just backed onto the set to couple up. (R. S. Carpenter/M. Hitches collection)

Darlington services. The experience gained with the sure-footedness of the 4-6-2Ts on the coast prompted Gresley to have H1 2162 rebuilt as a 4-6-2T in 1930, becoming the first A8. This loco was tested extensively over the former NER network and was found superior in every way to the 4-4-4Ts on the Whitby routes. Between May 1933 and August 1936, all the H1s were rebuilt as A8s at Darlington. The locos used in the Whitby area had slightly thinner boiler cladding, allowing room for the width of the water tanks to be increased, giving better endurance on the difficult coast lines with limited watering points. They remained the mainstay of these services until the arrival of the BR Standard Class

Whitby West Cliff Station

Gresley Class V3 tank locos, based at Middlesbrough, were used on passenger services over the coastal route to Scarborough from the late 1940s. (D. Blackwell collection)

Standard Class 4 2-6-4T 80119 was one of five such locomotives built at Brighton Works and delivered new to Whitby shed in 1955. (D. Blackwell collection)

Motive Power

A wealth of clues to the daily operational practices at West Cliff in the 1950s is present in this view of a Fairburn Tank taking water. The train will have arrived from Scarborough into the Middlesbrough-bound platform low on water. The driver has the injector on and is looking down from the cab window to see the water picking up – a clue that the boiler water level is low. Despite this, 42085 has run round the set before watering. This will have been to free the southbound platform for an imminent arrival from Middlesbrough. Note the signal behind the Abattoir Bridge is 'off' for the incoming train. To access the water crane it has been necessary to propel the set beyond the platform end and starting signal, towards the overrun. The short signal arm to the left of the loco is to authorise this move. (P. Hughes collection)

The Metropolitan-Camell Class 101 DMU sets were introduced after the WR&MUR had closed in May 1958, but were used extensively on the Whitby services for thirty years. (J. Lloyd collection)

4 2-6-4Ts in the mid-1950s and the DMUs at the end of that decade. During the Second World War, when trains on the coast route were shorter, the A8s were transferred away to other areas, returning again in peacetime.

The rebuilding of the H1s resulted in a temporary shortage of motive power, which in 1933 led to the use of J39 0-6-0s from Middlesbrough's Newport shed. The use of these heavier machines had to be specially authorised by the district engineer, but they were withdrawn following an incident on 9 August 1937, when 1449 spread the track at Prospect Hill. By this time, there were fifteen A8s available for use from the sheds serving the area: three at Whitby, three at Scarborough and nine at Middlesbrough.

After the Second World War, Class V1 and V3 2-6-2Ts from Middlesbrough shed began to work on the Scarborough trains. Under British Railways' North Eastern Region, weight restrictions south of Loftus were lifted, allowing the use of these heavier engines from 1949. A year later, Class L1 2-6-4Ts appeared – some of which were running in from Darlington works – followed by a former LMS Fairburn 2-6-4T, No. 42084, in April 1952.

The summer months of the mid-1950s saw tender engines on excursion trains, including Thompson B1s and ex-LMS Ivatt 4MT 2-6-0s. These trains generally worked south from Middlesbrough to Scarborough in the morning, returning in the evening full of day trippers homeward-bound from the resort towns. Some did not stop at all the intermediate stations, carrying express 'class one' head codes, an unusual sight on the WR&MUR.

By 1955, Whitby shed had received its allocation of five brand-new BR Standard Class 4 2-6-4Ts, fresh from Brighton Works, Nos 80116–80120, which were used on the coast service, replacing the earlier NER and LNER types. These remained in use in the Whitby area until the introduction of Metropolitan-Camell Class 101 DMUs in 1958, and worked the final trains over the WR&MUR in the May of that year. Indeed, it was number 80116 that hauled the last Middlesbrough to Scarborough passenger train of all, on 3 May 1958. This train left Middlesbrough at 16.20 with driver T. Southerland and fireman F. Appleton of Whitby shed in charge of the engine. Due to demand on the last day, the set was made up to five coaches at Middlesbrough and 80116 carried an improvised headboard lettered 'The Economist'.

Engine Sheds

Four engine sheds featured in the provision of locomotives for the Scarborough to Middlesbrough trains: at Whitby Town on the former Y&NMR, Saltburn on the S&DR extension, Middlesbrough and, to a lesser degree, Scarborough.

The first engine shed at Whitby was built by the Y&NMR in 1847, concurrently with the building of the present Town station. However, this was soon to prove too small for the growing demands, leading to an extension being built in 1867 at a cost of £1,500. Work on this had started in March of that year, but came to a halt in May when a local resident complained to the NER about the height of the new shed's roof. The design was altered and work completed the following year. The lower roof of the extension was brought to the height of the original during alterations in 1903, by which time the aggrieved resident must have moved on.

A 42-foot-long turntable was provided in the shed yard, but this was replaced in 1902 by a 50-foot table situated on the opposite side of the main line at Bog Hall. As locomotive types got larger, this was itself replaced by a 60-foot table on the same site in 1936.

Whitby shed provided the locos for passenger and local freight workings to Saltburn via the WR&MUR, Middlesbrough, along the Esk Valley and to Malton and Scarborough. The Sentinel railcars were kept here in the 1930s, which were used on the shuttle and short workings, but the passenger service was typically operated by heavy tank engines of class A6 and A8 4-6-2T, with smaller locos of class G5 on lighter workings. The pick-up goods trains were worked by 0-6-0 locos of classes J22, J23, J24, J25 and J27.

In 1955, the A6 and A8s were replaced by five new BR Standard Class 4 2-6-4Ts, which handled a majority of the traffic on the

Whitby West Cliff Station

WR&MUR in the final years. These were replaced by two Fairburn 2-6-4Ts and three Standard Class 3 2-6-0s, which were the final locos to be allocated to Whitby. The shed was closed with the introduction of DMUs on the Malton and Scarborough trains on 6 April 1959, but the building is still standing today.

Some typical allocations at Whitby were as follows:

1939:
LNER Class A6 4-6-2T. 686, 688, 689, 691, 692, 695
LNER Class A8 4-6-2T. 1523, 1527, 2155
LNER Class G5 0-4-4T. 1319, 1739, 1865
LNER Class J24 0-6-0. 1850, 1947
LNER Class J27 0-6-0. 1231
Sentinel Railcar. 2219 *New Fly*, 246 *Royal Sovereign*.

1954:
Ex-LNER Class A8 4-6-2T. 69860, 69861, 69864, 69865, 69888, 69890
Ex-LNER Class G5 0-4-4T. 67240, 67302
Ex-LNER Class J25 0-6-0. 65647, 65663, 65690

Following the S&DR's Saltburn extension in August 1861, it was decided to relocate their existing engine shed from Redcar to Saltburn. Approval for an expenditure of £350 was given in November 1863 for the construction of a building to house two locomotives – a tender being accepted for £411 13d 6s for its construction. In February the following year, it was decided to alter the design to allow four locos to be housed at a further cost of £250. The shed was extended again in 1877 to hold six engines.

However, on 17 April 1877, the roof of this shed was destroyed in a fire, damaging Class 901 No. 853, which was inside at the time. A new roof was built on the existing walls and the shed continued to be used until 27 January 1958, when DMUs were introduced on the Saltburn to Darlington trains and the shed was closed.

Through its working life, Saltburn shed was responsible for providing engines for the passenger services to Darlington and Scarborough. At the grouping in 1923, the Darlington trains were worked by NER Class D 4-4-4Ts (LNER H1), while the Scarborough trains were in the hands of Class W 4-6-2Ts (LNER A6), with smaller 0-4-4 BTPs for the autocar services. In May 1928, seven of Saltburn's H1s were exchanged

Engine Sheds

Former H&BR 0-6-0s of LNER Class J28 at Whitby shed yard in 1934, with the River Esk behind. These engines originally had domeless boilers. (R. S. Carpenter/M. Hitches collection)

An empty Whitby engine shed in the 1950s, squeezed between Esk Terrace on the left and the main lines on the right. Note the lovely NER water crane and the wider-spaced windows of the 1867 extension, visible through the open doors. (K. Hoole)

Whitby West Cliff Station

for A5 4-6-2s brought from Tyneside due to the H1's unsatisfactory performance on the Darlington trains. By June 1930, the remaining two H1s had been sent to Heaton. March 1939 saw the aging A5s replaced by seven new A8s, rebuilds of the original H1s, which proved very successful both on the Darlington and the WR&MUR services. Saltburn was eventually allocated nine of these versatile locomotives. Over the years the shed also housed various 0-6-0s for freight use and, in 1933, a Sentinel railcar was based here, for use on the Saltburn to Brotton service.

The allocation of engines at closure was as follows:

Ex-LNER Class A5 4-6-2. 69830, 69831, 69843, 69842
Ex-LNER Class A8 4-6-2. 69866, 69869

These locomotives were transferred to Middlesbrough on closure, but the shed yard remained in use for some years to come, to stand engines from visiting excursions. Some of Saltburn's engine shed buildings remain in industrial use today.

Middlesbrough shed provided engines for working the docks on the south bank of the River Tees and the numerous industrial concerns in

Saltburn engine shed was situated in the 'V' of the junction, formed where the Cleveland Railway's branch to Loftus diverged from the S&D Extension, north of Saltburn station. The Loftus line curved away on the embankment on the right. (K. Hoole)

A Class J25, from Whitby shed, at Newholm Beck viaduct in 1957. (A. Brown collection)

the area. After the northern terminus of the coast route to Scarborough was moved from Saltburn to Middlesbrough in 1933, locos were also provided for these trains. Typically, these were classes A6 and A8, with Gresley V1 and V3 tank engines appearing in later years.

Increasing traffic in the Teesside area saw Middlesbrough shed grow quickly from housing only four engines in 1845 to sixteen in 1854. By 1867, this in turn had become inadequate, leading to two new roundhouses being built, with a third added in 1872, holding around fifty-six engines at its peak. These roundhouses remained in use into the BR period, although bomb damage during the Second World War led to one being partly demolished, leaving the engines to stand around the turntable in the open air. By closure in 1959, the two remaining structures had become very run down and no trace of them exists today.

Whitby West Cliff Station

Following bomb damage during the Second World War, one of Middlesbrough's three roundhouses was demolished, and the others became increasingly run down as the 1950s progressed. Here we see seven of the sheds' residents, standing in the open air around the turntable of the demolished roundhouse in 1954, with a typical industrial Teesside backdrop. (K. Hoole)

An ex-LMS 8F at Scarborough shed. The tracks on which the engine stands were originally inside the straight shed, demolished following subsidence. (D. Blackwell collection)

LNER Class B17 on the turntable at Scarborough. (D. Blackwell collection)

A Class B12 outside Scarborough's straight shed. (D. Blackwell collection)

Whitby West Cliff Station

Scarborough loco shed was a much bigger concern than that at Whitby, providing as it did motive power for long-distance services, as well as accommodating the needs of much seasonal traffic; however, it did also house engines for use on the Whitby and Middlesbrough trains. A roundhouse was first authorised at Scarborough in 1879, at an estimated cost of £5,393 for the shed itself and an additional £2,976 for associated engineering works. The tender for its construction was let on 11 March 1880 for works at a cost of £4,330 8s 6d, with costs ultimately overrunning by £187 13s. Provision of a turntable added an additional £335 to the cost. An eight-road straight shed was opened in 1890, and the roundhouse fell into disuse, although it was used to store engines at times when there were sharp falls in traffic, especially during winter months.

In the early years, the coastal route to Whitby was worked by Scarborough's BTP 0-4-4Ts, followed by Worsdell Class O 0-4-4Ts. The Class W 4-6-0Ts specially built for this route were also housed at Scarborough in later NER days, both before and after their rebuilds as 4-6-2Ts under the LNER, as Class A6. The popular A8 tank engines were also Scarborough residents from the 1930s onwards.

During the 1950s, the east side wall of the straight shed had to be shored up due to subsidence. Eventually part of the shed was demolished, leaving the tracks on the south open to the elements. By this time, Scarborough's locomotive allocation was only eleven. The shed closed in May 1963, but the yard remained open for a further four years, providing water and turning facilities for locos from visiting excursions.

Evolution of NER Architecture

When the WR&MUR was opened by the NER in 1883, the steady expansion of route mileage under their control was coming to an end. By this time, they operated almost 600 passenger stations. The variety of their architectural styles reflected a company that had grown over the previous three decades through many amalgamations. Even those built by the NER itself showed different styles reflecting the dates built and the architects concerned. Although this rich variety of origin precluded there ever being a network-wide uniformity of design, by the time the WR&MUR came onto the scene there was an increasing standardisation of detail and appointment. This resulted in a recognisably 'North Eastern' appearance, which persisted long after the company ceased to exist.

After the formation of the NER in 1854, from the amalgamation of the Leeds Northern, York & North Midland and the York, Newcastle & Berwick Railways, a succession of company architects was appointed and it is possible to see their influence on subsequent building styles. The first to hold the post was Thomas Prosser, who introduced a simple rustic design for smaller country stations, with distinctive stepped gables. These were generally built from locally sourced materials. Examples can still be seen at Goathland and along the Esk Valley. This design was developed through the 1870s into an H-pattern building, which was to become almost standard for smaller stations built by the NER from this time onwards. These comprised a central block parallel to the running line, with short cross-wings at each end. In some instances, accommodation for the stationmaster was provided by a two-storey house on one cross-wing. The platform area between the projecting wings was generally covered by a sloping roof, supported on cast-iron columns. These were found across the NER system, with examples at Wensleydale, the Thirsk and Malton west of Pickering, Tyneside, and West Yorkshire. In a move towards greater standardisation, they generally paid little regard for the local vernacular, being mostly of red brick construction. This in itself was as a direct result of the success of the railways as national carriers, making a reliance on local building materials unnecessary.

This style was further developed by Prosser's successor in 1874, William Peachey, who held the office until 1877. On Peachey's resignation, the running of the architect's office passed to William Bell, who had served as Architect's Assistant under Peachey. During Bell's time as NER architect, most of the route mileage was in place and his work centred on extending and rebuilding many of the earlier stations due to increases in traffic and from the widening of major routes. Although the influence of his predecessor is evident in some of Bell's larger works, his smaller branch line stations tended to draw from the standard H-plan originated by Prosser. His interpretation of this design embodied a two-storey central block, with a flat for the stationmaster on the upper floor, flanked by single-storey wings. Its development can be followed through three lines, built between 1879 and 1883: the Swinton & Knottingley (1879), the Seamer & Pickering (1882) and the WR&MUR (1883).

The WR&MURs partly finished works were completed by the NER, with John Waddell's of Edinburgh securing the contract for the civil engineering. The construction of the station buildings was also entrusted to Waddell's, who secured the work by knocking 5 per cent off the price, to bring it into line with Bell's estimate. With the exception of West Cliff, all the stations were broadly similar to the Seamer & Pickering stations in the Forge Valley, with minor changes suggestive of the NER's readiness to spend a little extra money for decorative effect. It is likely that even at this early stage the NER were aware of the revenue-generating potential of Whitby as a resort and as such, were prepared to spend a little more.

The most obvious difference was in replacement of the bay window in the cross-wings by a broad window divided by mullions and a transom. These reflected the contemporary fashion in domestic architecture, in their use of large, plate glass sashes below the transom and small, glazed panes above it. All the openings had arched brick lintels, detailed with sandstone keystones and springers, unlike the Seamer & Pickering stations, with their plain, square tops. The walls were, in turn, detailed

Evolution of NER Architecture

Sawdon station, on the Seamer & Pickering's Forge Valley line of 1882, shows strong similarities to the later WR&MUR stations. The small hut with the row of fire buckets on the front housed the station's lever frame. The signal instruments were in the main station building. The WR&MUR stations all had more substantial platform signal boxes. (Lens of Sutton/M. Hitches collection)

A similar view of the WR&MUR's Hinderwell shows that the only major difference is the replacement of the bay windows with a broad window divided by mullions and a transom. In detail, the curved tops to the windows of the WR&MUR's station, replacing the square tops on the earlier stations, shows the NER's willingness to spend a little more for effect. The awning has been removed in this picture, but was originally identical to that of the other stations. Note that the chimney stacks have been heightened. A timber signal box has replaced the lever frame huts of the Forge Valley stations. (R. S. Carpenter/M. Hitches collection)

Whitby West Cliff Station

Typical window-top detail of the WR&MUR stations, this being at West Cliff. (P. Hughes)

This view of Staithes from the road approach shows how the cross-wings projected only a short distance at the back. The curved window tops are evident, as are the tall chimney stacks with stone detailing and capping. Note also the goods shed on the right, with its awning over the siding on the left and the cart dock on the right. All of these features were typical of William Bell's work on the WR&MUR stations. (R. S. Carpenter/M. Hitches collection)

with string courses of blue brick, similar to Bell's earlier stations. West Cliff used the same detailing elements as the other WR&MUR stations, providing an obvious continuity, but it departed from the later H-plan design, in that it provided a two-storey house for the stationmaster in one wing, with the other having a single story. In this way, it can be seen to lend more to the original Prosser stations in Wensleydale than to the later Forge Valley type. It bears strong similarities to Bell's stations on the Tynemouth Extension of 1882.

Hence, the stations employed on the WR&MUR represent the end product of thirty years of building and evolution through the hands of three architects. With the NER network all but complete by 1883, the need for further development of this design of wayside station had vanished.

A Walk Around Whitby West Cliff Station

It is appropriate to start our tour of West Cliff station with the goods facilities, as it was from this side that most passengers to the station will have approached. The goods yard was located at the north-east side of the station site, with coal cells flanking the right boundary and a handling warehouse and loading dock behind the Down platform, parallel to the running lines.

Almost all NER stations had goods-handling facilities of some sort, with the supply of domestic coal being a common thread. Local business will have influenced the nature of facilities provided to some degree, with many goods-handling yards expanding and contracting as the nature of local trade developed. By the 1880s, the NER was well established as a provider of goods-handling facilities and had already developed a range of adaptable structures and equipment to meet this demand.

The track layout of the goods yard followed a straightforward arrangement, fanning out from a single facing connection under the abattoir bridge. Two sidings led to the goods shed area, flanking both sides of the open loading dock, with one extending in front of the warehouse, totalling 90 and 160 yards respectively. A third siding ran up the ramp to the coal depots, 155 yards in length, with 117 yards of available standage, including a short loop of 93 yards to allow coal wagons to be run around, as locomotives were not normally permitted to pass over the cells.

For many years, goods sheds at smaller stations tended to follow the Thomas Prosser design, providing a single track shed with a loading platform within the building and wide doors on the rear wall, allowing a cart to be reversed into the shed area for loading. This developed into a more economical structure under the guidance of William Bell.

A Walk Around Whitby West Cliff Station

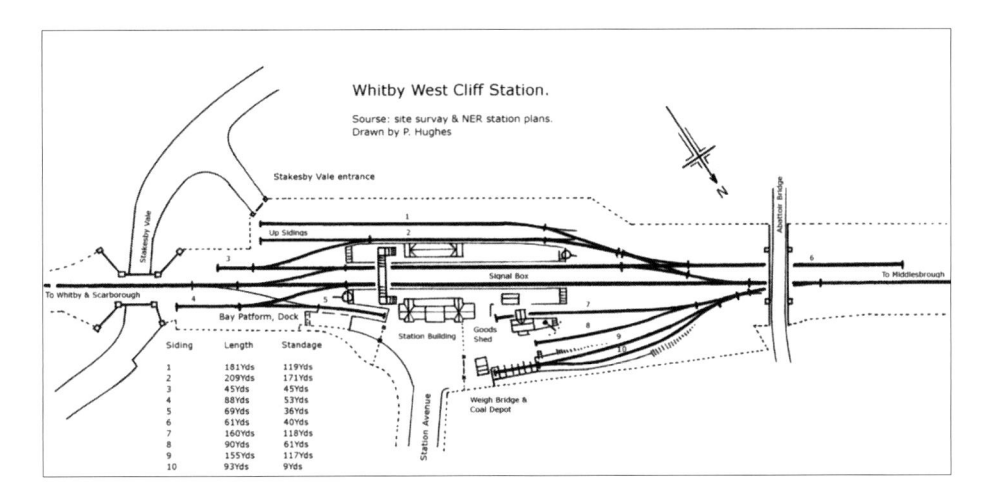

Whitby West Cliff Station.
Sourse: site survay & NER station plans.
Drawn by P. Hughes

Siding	Length	Standage
1	181Yds	119Yds
2	209Yds	171Yds
3	45Yds	45Yds
4	88Yds	53Yds
5	69Yds	36Yds
6	61Yds	40Yds
7	160Yds	118Yds
8	90Yds	61Yds
9	155Yds	117Yds
10	93Yds	9Yds

The first example of this type of building appeared at Riding Mill, where the directors asked Bell to provide a cheaper alternative to the then standard design. This was achieved by leaving the track outside the building, resulting in a neat, roofed loading platform. This design evolved quickly and by the 1880s was being used across the NER system at smaller stations as far afield as Alnwick, Wearhead and Copmanthorpe.

This pattern of goods shed was used at all the WR&MUR stations, with the addition of a small outside loading dock equipped with a crane. The sheds featured a cantilevered awning over the railway with wooden valancing, curved to match the loading gauge. The rear wall included a cart dock, covered by a small veranda formed by extending the line of the roof downwards on lengthened trusses. These were supported by diagonal timber beams, set into the wall over sandstone keys. All the WR&MUR sheds were built from the same red brick as the main station buildings, with the recessed panels and detailing typical of Bell's approach. Window sills and window and door lintels were of dressed sandstone, linking visually with those employed on the main buildings. Heavy wooden sliding doors were provided on the road and railway sides, running on cast-iron wheels to support their weight and ease opening. These ran on metal rails set into the floor and mounted as runners on the wall above. A third, smaller sliding door gave access from the inside loading area onto the dock, which was included on the WR&MUR sheds, extending towards the rail entrance of the siding. On earlier sheds, without the additional dock area, a window occupied this position.

The dock was provided with a hand-operated crane, with a lifting capacity of 1.5 tons. These cranes were not built by the NER themselves, but were bought in from a variety of manufactures, including I'Anson, Whessoe Grays and Cowen Sheldon. The WR&MUR cranes originated from the latter and, as such, will have been found in a variety of industrial locations, as well as in railway use. The cranes were serviced periodically throughout their working lives by staff from the original manufacturer.

One of the most distinctive features of NER stations was the use of coal cells, referred to as depots, provided to allow coal to be deposited from bottom-emptying wagons directly into compartments, or cells, beneath the tracks. From here it was loaded onto coal merchants' carts and weighed prior to leaving the yard. Almost every NER station featured a coal depot of some sort.

In order to gain the height required over the cells, the siding at West Cliff led up a short ramp with the road level dropped to gain the necessary clearance, a common arrangement for these depots. The cell walls were built of large stone blocks, as opposed to the brick used for the rest of the station. This was necessary to withstand the weight of fully loaded coal wagons over these 2-foot-thick walls. They were arranged at 12-foot centres, with six cells in total at West Cliff. The number of cells varied from depot to depot, with some larger stations having many, often provided with multiple tracks. The bases of the cell walls were protected from damage from cart wheels, by the use of large, stone rubbing blocks. The siding over the cells was carried on either timber weigh-beams with bull-head rails, or on deep webbed-girder rails, the upper flange of which was profiled as a running rail. Both arrangements were used in the Whitby area, with the surviving depots at Goathland on the North Yorkshire Moors Railway using modified girder rails, while those at West Cliff used timber beams. A wooden walkway was provided at each side of the track over the depots, with a wooden handrail and steps at the end nearest the station for access.

The roadways alongside the coal depots were paved with stone sets, while the goods yard areas were properly made up and drained, with tarmac surfaces edged with sleepers to the level of the siding rail heads. Surfaces of passenger platforms on many smaller stations were of packed ash, often with only areas in front of buildings or entrances having hard surfaces. Many retained this feature until their closure, but West Cliff's platforms were finished with tarmac surfaces from new.

A Walk Around Whitby West Cliff Station

The goods shed at West Cliff, after closure. The cart dock was accessed through sliding doors located where the steps are. An awning shielded the loading area; the stone keys for this are still visible at either side of the door in the centre. (P. Hughes)

A weighbridge was located adjacent to the end of the cells, a small brick structure detailed with blue courses, stone sills and lintels. The weighing equipment was provided by Pooley of Wolverhampton and, like the crane, the weigh tables were serviced by their manufacturer's staff throughout their working lives. The weighbridge building differs architecturally from the other West Cliff buildings, indicating that it is in fact designed by Pooley themselves. It was common practice for the weighbridge to be installed by Pooley and, where they were separate from the main station buildings, the associated building would be of their design. The type found at West Cliff was typical of those adopted in this part of North Yorkshire, with similar

Whitby West Cliff Station

examples found on all the lines around Whitby and Scarborough. That the West Cliff building is constructed from the same brick as the main station buildings suggests it was built concurrently with the other structures and may have been constructed by Waddells, to the Pooley design.

The weighing equipment was serviced throughout its working life by Pooley's and the machines carried both Pooley and NER identification number plates. In the mid-1990s, the machine from the WR&MUR station at Hinderwell was recovered for restoration and use at the preserved Goathland station. During this project, it was found that the Pooley identification plate had been attached before the machine was painted, at an early stage of manufacture. However, the NER plate was fitted after painting and is likely to have been fitted after the machine was installed. There was evidence of only one coat of paint during the life of the machine, hence the colours found at restoration

The coal cells at West Cliff. The NER always referred to these facilities as 'depots'. The number of individual cells varied from place to place, the six here being typical of a station of this size. In some rural locations, covered cells were provided for lime delivery. West Cliff handled all the coal traffic for Whitby, as no coal facilities were provided at the Town station until the late 1960s, after West Cliff had closed. Note the weighbridge to the right and a typical cast-iron NER buffer stop on the end of the siding to the left. (N. Cholmondeley collection)

A Walk Around Whitby West Cliff Station

The extant weighbridge at Wykeham is identical to that at West Cliff. The Pooley weighing machine remains inside and the table lies hidden under the gravel. This building is on private property, but can be easily seen from a nearby road. (P. Hughes)

were those originally used. The main colour was a dark Brunswick green, with black panels on the weigh arm and the ornamental bracket picked out in red. Photographic and anecdotal evidence suggests this was a standard scheme used by Pooley, as examples in West Yorkshire, Tyneside and as far afield as Western Region have been found to be similarly treated.

Although the weighbridge at West Cliff was demolished after closure, some similar structures still exist in the area. A good example can be found at Wykeham on the Forge Valley line, surviving along with its scale, and is identical to the structure at West Cliff.

Whitby West Cliff Station

However, the coal cells themselves survived in an overgrown and derelict condition until the site was redeveloped in 2002. Some of the large sandstone blocks were removed in the years after closure, presumably to be used in building elsewhere. The goods shed was converted to act as a builders' merchant's office, losing its awnings and gaining an extension over the dock, but retaining many of its original features. This too was demolished in 2002. The identical shed at Sandsend was used for many years as a boat-building workshop, operated by Tony Goodall, son of the Sandsend stationmaster Albert Goodall. This stood until the mid-1990s, but has now also been demolished to make way for road alterations and a doctors' surgery. The only surviving goods shed from the WR&MUR today is that at Staithes.

The main station building at West Cliff was appreciably larger than its WR&MUR counterparts on the intermediate stations. Its layout shows a strong link to the earlier Prosser design of wayside station found in Wensleydale and west of Pickering, in that a single-storey centre section of the H-plan is flanked at the north end by a two-storey house and yard for the stationmaster, with a single-story office block at the other end. The family resemblance to the other WR&MUR stations, and indeed to their predecessors in the Forge Valley, is strong, due to Bell's consistent use of standard features such as chimney stack design, proportion of door and window apertures and the use of blue brick and sandstone detailing. The proportions of the building, in terms of gable pitch and overall heights are consistent with the other WR&MUR stations. Indeed, such was Bell's standardisation of approach by this time that these features can be found on other examples of his work as far afield as Tyneside and Stockton, forging a strong NER identity across the company.

Approaching the station from the Station Avenue direction, as most passengers will have done, we are faced with a dignified hip-roofed booking hall pavilion, with a small awning spanning the entrance and the windows at either side. The booking hall was set forward from the flanking single-story office blocks, to increase its impact as an entrance, while the composition was neatly bookended by gabled wings. The stationmaster's house was formed from two two-story, gable-ended blocks at right angles, with an enclosed yard at the northern end. The southern wing was comprised of a single-story, gable-ended block, housing a ladies' waiting area and toilets, the lower part of its window opening being bricked up. A ventilator was provided in the roof, similar

A Walk Around Whitby West Cliff Station

The view from Station Road, with the goods yard to the left. Note the railway lamp standard, minus its head, on the approach road. (N. Cholmondeley collection)

to that above the gentlemen's toilet in the flanking block on the north side of the booking hall and that in the building on the northbound platform.

In line with the other WR&MUR stations and Bell's work on the Forge Valley, these cross-wings projected further outwards on the platform side, bridged by a sloping awning supported on six cast-iron columns. The booking hall stood higher than the level of the awning, with its eaves embellished with brick detail, which supported cast-iron guttering. The flanking office blocks had their eaves in line with the top of the awning, with a simplified form of the booking hall's embellishment. The columns supporting the awning were hollow and doubled as rainwater down pipes, giving a neat finish, uncluttered by drain pipes. Tall, ornamental chimney stacks, with sandstone detailing and cappings topped by neat, square pots, completed the High Victorian picture.

That the NER were prepared to spend a little more on West Cliff than on the intermediate stations highlights its status in what was, by the 1880s, a growing and fashionable area of a prospering town. Sited at an interchange of routes in a ballooning resort, significant numbers of travellers were anticipated.

This is evidenced by the wide platform area provided in front of the main block. Strong similarities can be seen with Bell's stations on

Whitby West Cliff Station

The booking hall pavilion in the 1990s. The position of the awning can be seen from the cleaner brickwork over the door and adjacent windows as well as the stone key blocks. The awning was removed from West Cliff after closure, but a similar feature has recently been reinstated at William Bell's Tynemouth station. (P. Hughes)

the North Tyne Loop, at Cullercoats and, on a much grander scale, Tynemouth, which dated from 1882, preceded West Cliff by just a year. These stations were also provided with wide platform areas to accommodate crowds of arriving and returning day trippers and commuters. Cullercoats, like Whitby, was situated on the coast and was becoming a popular destination with visitors from industrial Tyneside, much as Whitby was from Middlesbrough and West Yorkshire. The architectural themes identified as typical of Bell's work are evident in both these buildings, as the frontage of the main building at Cullercoats is almost identical to that at West Cliff.

A Walk Around Whitby West Cliff Station

Unlike West Cliff, Cullercoats remains in railway use today; although it has now lost its two-storey stationmaster's house, leaving a rather unbalanced and foreshortened structure, it retains some details lost at West Cliff. A study of the frontage of Cullercoats, considered along with the surviving stationmaster's house at West Cliff, gives a reasonable impression of how both stations appeared when new. Details such as the ticket windows remaining in the booking hall at Cullercoats have been long lost at West Cliff. On the platform side, Cullercoats differed significantly, in that Bell had provided glazed, free-standing canopies as opposed to an awning.

After closure in 1961, West Cliff spent a period of time standing empty before the site was cleared. The main building was used for many years after this as offices by Yorkshire Water. While the nature of changes made internally during this time are unknown, externally, apart from the blocking up of some windows and closing in the front of the canopy on the former platform side, little change was made until 2001, when it was redeveloped as housing.

This 1908 view, looking north, shows the platform side of the main building to good effect. Note the awning on cast columns, which doubled as rainwater drain pipes for a less cluttered effect. Under the awning is a typical collection of NER station furniture, including benches, a clock, poster boards and a portable weighing machine. (N. Cholmondeley collection)

Whitby West Cliff Station

Across the tracks on the Middlesbrough-bound platform was provided a long, thin waiting shelter built from red brick and wood. Although linking visually with the main building and the other WR&MUR stations, it is possible this structure may have been unique. To some extent, its form will have been governed by the constraints of the site on which it was built, as it was restricted in available width by sidings behind and in turn by the Co-op Creamery beyond the railway boundary. A sufficiently sized waiting area will have been required for returning day trippers to Teesside, while the east-facing location will have been exposed at this time, bearing in mind that the West Cliff area of town will have been more open when the station was built.

William Bell's solution to this brief was to provide a long, partly open-fronted waiting area flanked by gable-ended blocks at each end, providing toilet facilities and office space. The outer blocks were both wider and higher than the waiting area in between, but the proportions of their gables were identical, with roof ridges in line longitudinally.

The block at the north end provided a gent's toilet, entered through a screened door in the gable end. The ladies' room was provided in the main building. A door in the front wall of the north block led into an area probably originally used as a ticket office. Traces of a bricked-up ticket window were evident in the wall adjoining the central waiting area after closure, suggesting this area was indeed once a secondary ticket office and its associated storeroom.

The proportions and detailing of the windows and doors in the end blocks were identical to those of the main building, with courses of blue brick providing further continuity. It is likely that these flanking blocks will have been planned to be identical, with the exception of a window in place of the door in the south gable. However, as finally built, the south block was altered to give an open-fronted waiting area with a stove on the rear wall for heating. The roof was supported by a wooden beam under the eaves, which was later further supported with a central tubular upright. It is likely that, at some point in the LNER period, the window in the south gable was enlarged, creating a long, rectangular opening with aluminium window frames, which harshly contrasted with the existing station architecture. Although an exact date for this alteration is unknown, the building materials used suggest the 1930s – 1934 being likely – as this was when the loading dock was rebuilt as a platform to accommodate the Whitby Town shuttle service.

A Walk Around Whitby West Cliff Station

Although long after closure, the diagonal boarding is evident in this 1990s view. Originally, all the upper windows were divided into four panes. (P. Hughes)

Bench seating was provided inside the open waiting area, fixed to the walls in a similar manner to that in the central block. The brick walls inside this area were painted white, with the wall space used for poster boards.

The central waiting area between the two flanking blocks was divided at its midpoint, the southern portion being open fronted, while the remainder was enclosed by attractive, glazed, wooden screens, with diagonal boarding to their lower sections. These were similar in appearance to other such lightweight wooden works found on NER waiting rooms and train shed ends and was similar to that of West Cliff's signal box. The glazing style mirrored that of the larger station windows and current domestic fashion, in that large, glazed panes were provided below a wooden transom, with small, square panes above. Inside, bench seating was fixed to the walls, with poster boards on the rear brick wall. Heating was provided from coal fires with chimney

Whitby West Cliff Station

A column from the front of the open waiting area. (P. Hughes)

A Walk Around Whitby West Cliff Station

Typical window details. Traces of where a poster board was fixed are visible on the wall to the right. The datum post was below the window on the left. (P. Hughes)

Bench seating along with green and cream paintwork in the waiting area. (P. Hughes)

Whitby West Cliff Station

The waiting rooms after closure. Note the vent in the roof of the former gent's toilet and the decorative finials on the gables. (P. Hughes)

stacks identical to those of the main building. The open area, at the south end, was separated from the enclosed part by a wood and glass screen of identical appearance to those on the front, with a single door.

The datum post, a rectangular cast plate bearing the letters 'DP', was located below the windows of the northern block. These datum posts were used for route-measurement purposes, installed from around 1900 and usually located at the midpoint of the Down platform on all NER stations. At West Cliff, with the directional terminology reversed,

A Walk Around Whitby West Cliff Station

The waiting rooms on the Up platform are visible behind this Fairburn tank, which has just run into the station. The guard has climbed down onto the track and appears to be walking to the rear of the train, to take off the tail lamp and drop down the vacuum bag. The wooden screen around the gent's toilet door is visible to the right of the loco. (N. Cholmondeley collection)

it was located here on the Up patform. Most were mounted on a short post, but at West Cliff it was fixed directly to the wall.

This building also survived closure, and a long period in use as storage by Yorkshire Water, basically intact. Most of the front of the building was enclosed by a wood and corrugated sheet lean-to, but most of the internal features remained. Like the main station building, this structure remains in use today, with the two flanking blocks being converted into flats, pleasingly matching the original architecture of the building, and replacing the open front in a style closely matching that of the original. The covered waiting area now gives protection to cars, but the glazed screens have been lost.

The signal boxes provided on the WR&MUR were of a type unique to the NER system and, as such, it is possible they may have originated from the contractors who supplied the signalling equipment themselves. The NER favoured equipment from the Worcestershire manufacturer McKenzie & Holland and early photographs indicating their distinctive signals were used from the start. However, the boxes show no direct lineage to link them to other McKenzie designs either, leading them to be termed as 'unclassified' in the Signalling Study Group's definitive survey. They were all built contemporary with the other station buildings by Waddell's.

Hence, these boxes appear to be unique to the WR&MUR, totalling six examples: West Cliff, Sandsend, Kettleness, Hinderwell, Staithes and Grinkle. They all followed a standard wooden modular construction, allowing variations in size, and were all platform-mounted structures. They featured ornate barge boards on the gable ends and diagonal boarding below the windows, arranged symmetrically. The six-by-two pattern and size of the sliding sashes bears close similarities with those found on the NER S1 pattern signal boxes. Wood had rarely been used by the NER in signal box construction up to this time, unless its lighter weight made it necessary due to unstable ground. However, in the following years it was used much more frequently as the NER expanded and updated existing installations, offering savings in cost and construction times. On the rear wall was a brick panel flanking the stove and stovepipe provided for heating. Unusually, the pipe was routed up the inside of the roof and out through the ridge line. This gave the impression from the outside that the stove was in the middle of the floor. In some cases, the stoves were relocated at the front if lever frames were renewed at the rear of the operating floor during the LNER period. At some point in the life of West Cliff signal box, a crude storm porch was added to protect the door in the south-facing gable end. Storm porches were not a common feature on southern division boxes and, as such, it is likely this was a local alteration.

The lower part of the building, hidden below platform level, was of brick construction, as were the sides of the rodding duct through the platform. The rodding duct was covered by substantial timber boards, allowing the platform to be continued in front of the box. These were removable for maintenance. Access to the locking room, housing the

A Walk Around Whitby West Cliff Station

The wooden signal box on the Down platform around 1959. The Class 101 DMU will have travelled from Scarborough and is about to depart for Whitby Town station, having changed direction. The DMU's destination blind reads 'Whitby', not 'Whitby Town'. All the DMU blinds were lettered in this way. Note the new upper-quadrant advanced starting signal, visible beyond the bridge, installed when the station became a terminus in 1958. (N. Cholmondeley collection)

lower part of the lever frame, interlocking and the mechanical lead-off, was via a trap door in the operating floor. A pit below the level of the locking room gave access to the undersides of the fixings securing the crank and pulley stands. Drainage was usually provided from these pits by stone soakaways. The brick outline of the locking room was visible at West Cliff until the site was redeveloped in 2002. Taller structures differed in that their locking rooms could be entered through a door at ground level.

All the WR&MUR boxes, except for Staithes, were mounted on the Down (Whitby-bound) platforms, at a midpoint respective to the

Whitby West Cliff Station

Though smaller, the other WR&MUR signal boxes were of the same style as West Cliff. By the time this picture was taken of Kettleness, the lever frame had been moved to the back. Only West Cliff retained its lever frame at the front. The wooden cabinet to the left of the signal box, will have housed batteries associated with the token machines and the electrical interlocking of the lever frame. (R. S. Carpenter/M. Hitches collection)

ends of the passing loops. This was to maximise loop length, as facing points could only be worked mechanically over a distance of around 200 yards.

When new, all the WR&MUR signal boxes had their lever frames at the front of the operating floor, following standard practice of the day. However, by closure only West Cliff retained this feature, as the others had their frames relocated to the rear. This was LNER practice from the 1920s onwards, leaving the front windows unobstructed and also allowing the new lever frame to be installed before the old one was removed. That these boxes all had this feature suggests they had their frames replaced early in the LNER period. Records of frames provided

A Walk Around Whitby West Cliff Station

since 1927 by the York S&T workshops, from the collection of former signalling engineer John Boyes, show no mention of the WR&MUR boxes, indicating replacement was likely to have been before this date.

At closure, West Cliff had a 35-lever McKenzie & Holland pattern 16 frame, of 5-inch centres. It is possible this was an early replacement of an original, older frame, as pattern 16 frames tended not to be used in the area until around the turn of the century. The length of the signal box was considerably greater than the 18-foot 4-inch length of the pattern 16 frame, raising the possibility that there may indeed have been a longer frame before this one. Older frames tended to have levers spaced further apart than later examples, typically at 6-inch centres. The later McKenzie & Holland frames favoured by the NER and LNER had lever centres of 4 or 5 inches. During the course of the frame's working life, it was re-locked three times, reflecting changes in the track layout and station usage.

The first came around 1910, as we have seen, to facilitate the reversal of the Whitby Town to Scarborough trains in the Middlesbrough-bound platform. This involved some alteration of the levers controlling points at the south end, to allow the facing point locks to be worked. A new starting signal was installed at the south end of this platform, which may have been recovered and reused from elsewhere. The Up and Down distant signals were permanently fixed at caution at this time and lever 35, which had formerly worked the Down distant, was used to operate the new signal.

The next change came in 1934, as a result of the conversion of the loading dock at the south end to a passenger bay to accommodate the Whitby Town shuttle service. This was part of a series of signalling and operational improvements carried out by the LNER at this time to improve line capacity on the whole of the Middlesbrough to Scarborough route. By providing the Whitby Town shuttle with its own platform, the Middlesbrough to Scarborough trains were free to use the two main platforms to pass on the single line. This therefore maximised line capacity for trains on the coast service during the busy summer timetable.

The rarely used loading dock at the south end of the Scarborough-bound platform was lengthened with a timber extension to give room for two coaches. The track layout and signalling were altered to allow Up trains to run directly into the new bay platform from the main running line. This was achieved through the addition of a new facing

Whitby West Cliff Station

The south end starting signals are visible in this view dating from around 1960. The bay platform is on the left. Note the new advanced starting signal, No. 15, in the centre between the two buffer stops and Prospect Hill's distant on the LNER lattice and tubular steel post. West Cliff's Down starter, No. 32, is above this signal, obscured by the bridge spandrel. This post replaced an earlier NER wooden signal. (N. Cholmondeley collection)

connection. It is interesting that the Up home signal, No. 3, which controlled access to the Up (Middlesbrough-bound) platform or the bay, showed no route indication. The reason for this is unclear, but may have been a result of having no convenient spare levers available to work an additional arm, or possibly as a cost-saving measure. Anecdotal evidence suggests the Whitby Town shuttle would be brought to a stand at No. 3 signal, with the points set to the Up platform. Then the route was reset to the bay and the signal cleared, proving via mechanical detection that the facing points were correctly set. This practice is in line with signalling regulations, requiring a clearing point (safety overlap) ahead of the home signal, to be maintained clear until the approaching train is at a stand. Accepting all Up trains with the route set to Up platform, irrespective of whether the train requires the bay, provided flank protection, ensuring any overrun of No. 3 signal would not conflict with a correctly signalled Down train. The track diagrams illustrate how this was achieved, with overrun trapping at the ends off both platform lines. This allowed trains to be signalled to enter both platforms simultaneously if required. Both overruns were originally also signalled and used as head shunts to access the respective goods sidings and the dock. However, the signal to the Down overrun appears to have been removed in the early British Railways period. By this time, the loading dock had been used as a passenger bay for many years and the overrun's use as a storage siding will have been limited by its short length.

Further changes took place in May 1958, when the WR&MUR line to Saltburn was closed. After this time, West Cliff served as a terminus, with the route severed at the bridge under Upgang Lane, to the north of the station. The remaining stub of the WR&MUR acted as a long siding and head shunt, used to access the goods yard and run round trains. The signalling was altered to reflect this. The track diagram illustrates how the goods yard point controls were altered to provide both platform lines with protection from runaways in this new siding, as well as changes to the signals at both ends.

The Whitby Town shuttles were discontinued at this time, the service being provided by the Whitby–Scarborough DMU trains, introduced from May 1958. The former bay platform retained its facing connection, but reverted to use as a loading dock. At this time, signalling at the south end was revised to give the dock its own signal at last, No. 6, which had formerly been the Up advanced starter; made redundant with the station's closure as a through route. A new Down advanced starter was provided, reflecting the need to shunt into the Prospect Hill section to run trains round.

No further changes were made to the signalling arrangements in the following three years up to the point of closure in 1961. The signal box closed on 11 May 1961, a day after the station was closed to passengers. This will have allowed any remaining stock to be removed from the sidings, before the track was taken into possession of the District Engineers Department. The signal box was the first structure at the station to be demolished post-closure, after standing derelict for around ten years. Similar fates befell many redundant signal boxes, as their small sizes and unique features did not lend themselves well to other uses.

Whitby West Cliff Station

The signal box, looking north. The diagonal boarding below the windows and the ornate barge boards are displayed to good effect, as is the storm porch. A number of telegraph posts can be seen behind the building. On the NER, telegraph posts were sited on the Up side of the running line, except where they needed to cross for operational reasons. Mile posts and gradient boards, on the other hand, were always on the Down side. (N. Cholmondeley collection)

Shunting at Kettleness. The signalman is about to hand over the token. (J. M. Boyes collection)

A Walk Around Whitby West Cliff Station

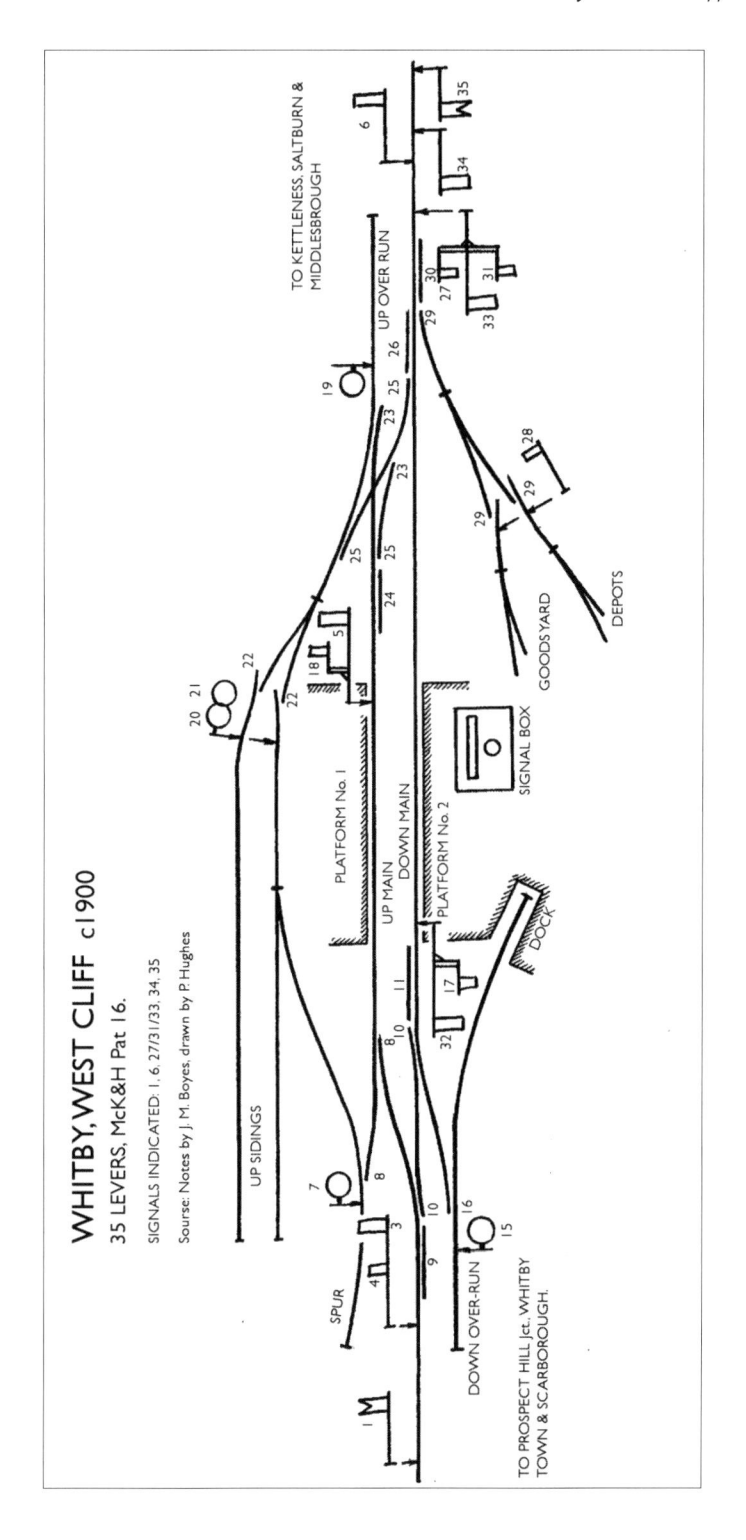

Whitby West Cliff Station

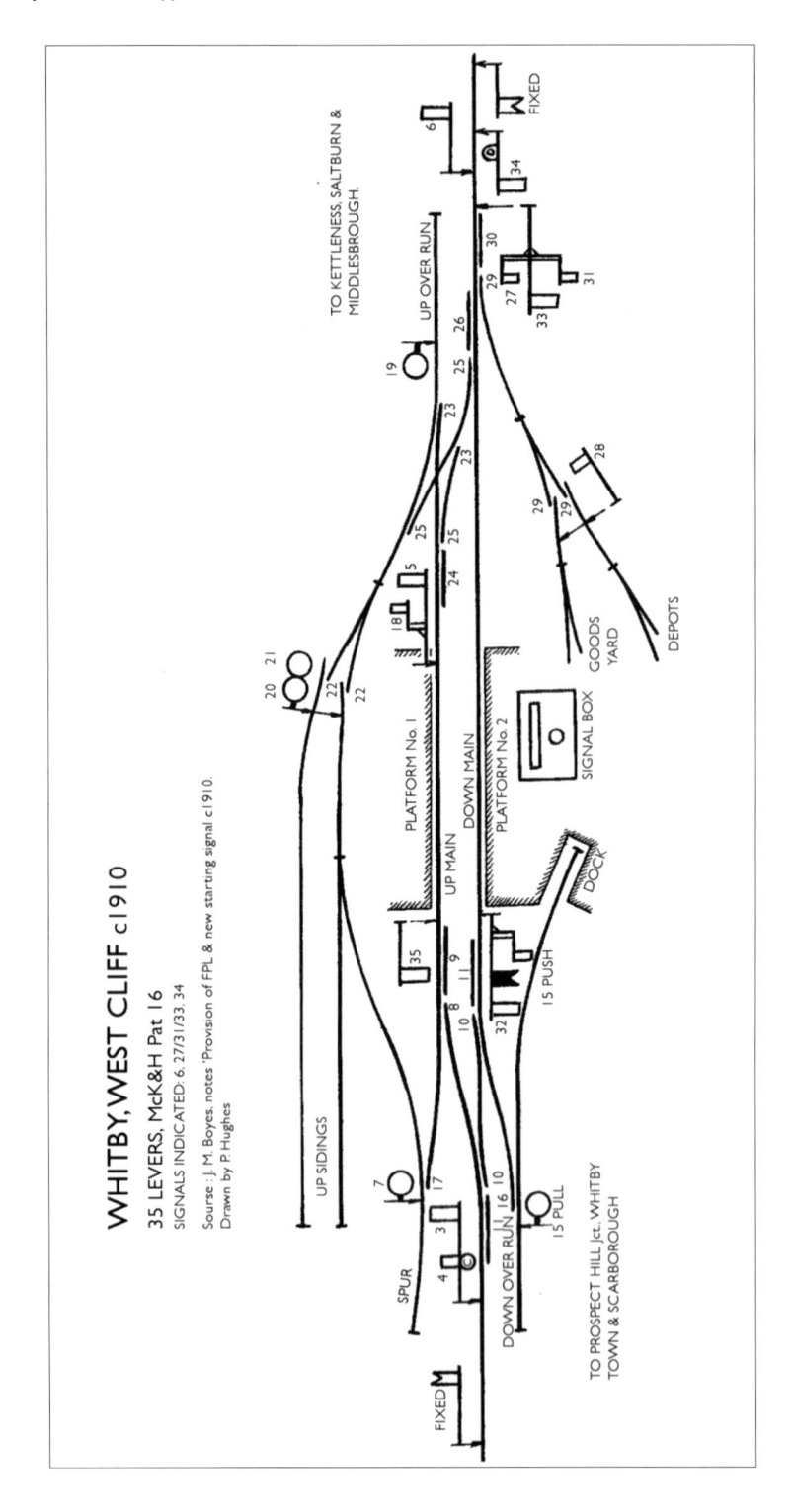

A Walk Around Whitby West Cliff Station

WHITBY, WEST CLIFF 1951
35 LEVERS, McK&H PAT 16

SIGNALS INDICATED: 6, 14, 27/31/33, 34
SIGNAL LIGHTS INDICATED: 6, 34, UP DISTANT, DOWN DISTANT

Source: Site survey 6 July 1951, from the collection of J. M. Boyes.
Drawn by P. Hughes

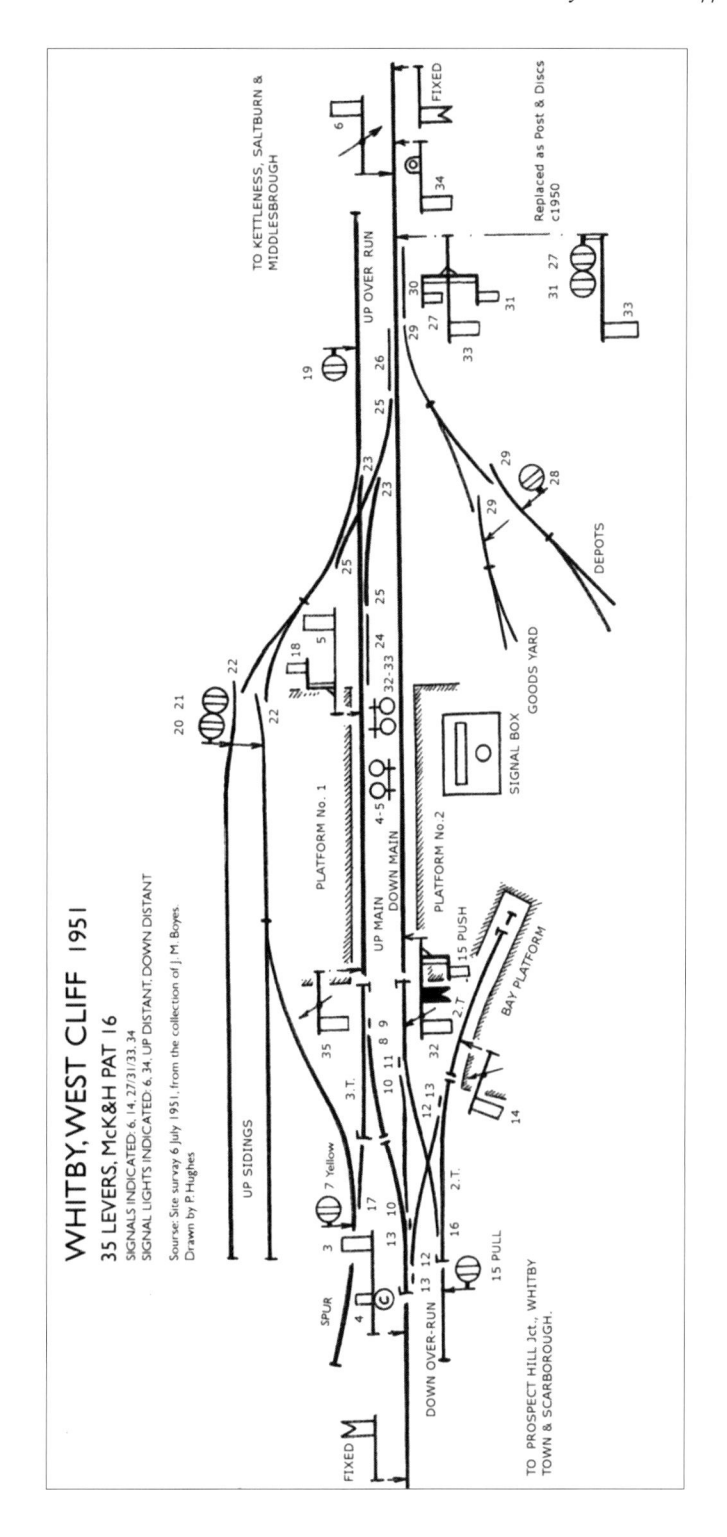

Whitby West Cliff Station

WHITBY, WEST CLIFF 1959
35 LEVERS, McK&H PAT 16

SIGNALS INDICATED: 14, 15, 20, 21, 27/31, 33/34
SIGNAL LIGHTS INDICATED: 15, 27/31, 33/34, UP DISTANT

Source: Site survey by J. M. Boyes. 30 September 1959
Drawn by P. Hughes

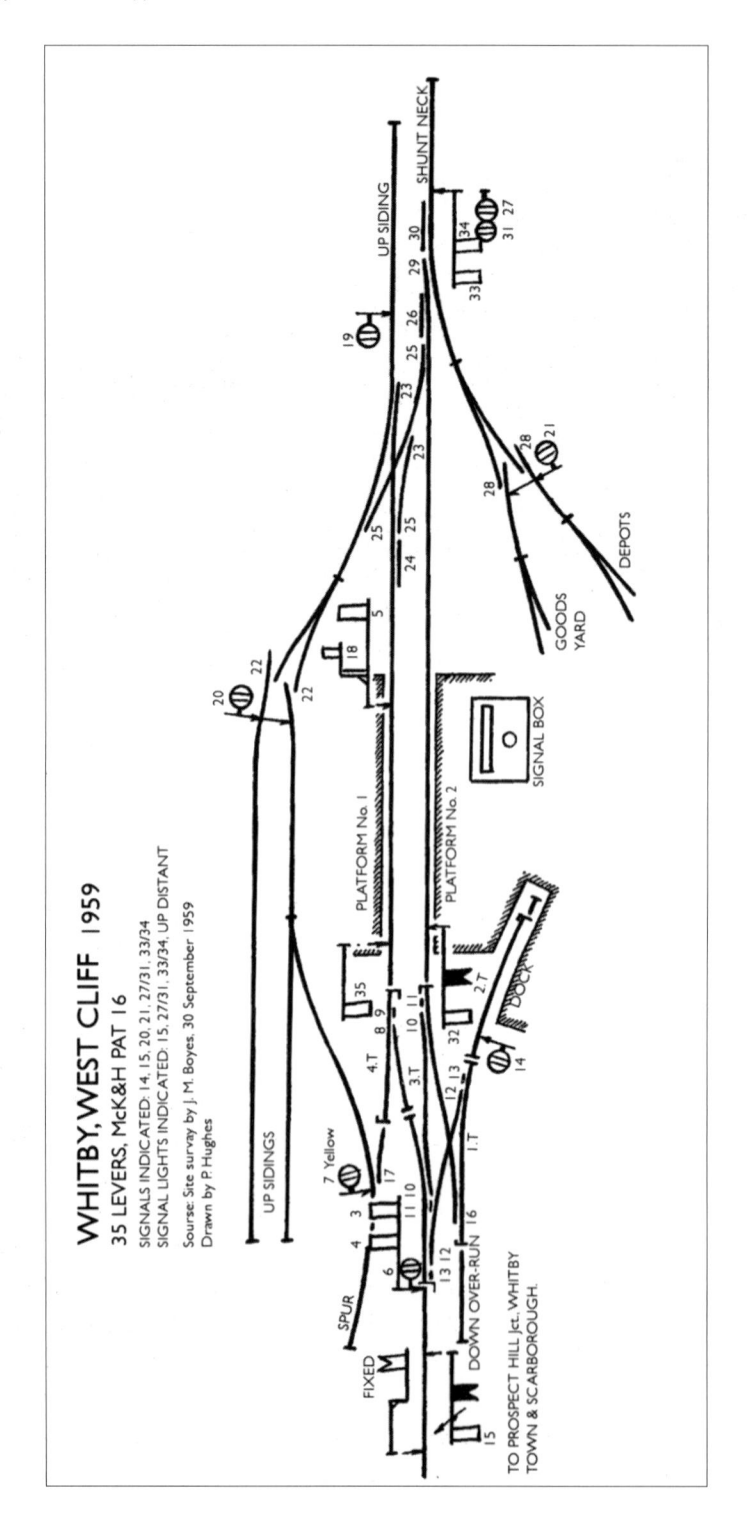

A Walk Around Whitby West Cliff Station

By the early 1970s, all of the track had gone, but behind the rubble the station buildings and signal box still stand. The area between the platforms is filled in. (N. Cholmondeley collection)

Signal boxes were generally demolished into their pits, the rubble effectively filling the hole. None of the former WR&MUR's unique signal boxes now survive.

West Cliff's intended use as an interchange station, with passengers swapping trains and platforms to access stations along the two routes that crossed at Whitby, was reflected in the provision of a footbridge from new. None of the other stations on the coast route from Saltburn to Scarborough, or the Whitby to Malton line, featured bridges. This is indicative of the optimism that the Victorian planners held for the development of Whitby as a resort, due to the arrival of the railway and the traffic levels they anticipated. In reality, West Cliff was probably only busy enough to fully justify a bridge during the summer months. Its provision, and the wide platform area outside the main buildings, is similar to the contempory coastal stations on the North Tyne Loop, also designed to accommodate anticipated large numbers of visitors arriving in early morning and leaving around tea time.

Whitby West Cliff Station

A final view looking north from the signal box window. The date will be around 1967, as the platforms have not yet been filled in. The stone bridge in the background, which gave access to the abattoir, was later blocked up. (N. Cholmondeley collection)

A Walk Around Whitby West Cliff Station

A useful view of the bridge, with a Class A8 loco taking water in the Down platform. The signage appears to date from the LNER period. (N. Cholmondeley collection)

The NER started to evolve a standard design of station footbridge in the early 1870s, the prototype of which still exists at Monkwearmouth in Sunderland. This design, fabricated from steel plate, evolved over a number of years into the more familiar cast-iron version, which saw use across the NER system from around 1891, totalling around fifty examples. Many of these bridges remain today.

The West Cliff footbridge, No. 70, shows a clear resemblance to the later standard cast structures, but dating as it did from 1883, pre-dates the classic design by almost ten years. The curved spandrels, incorporating the bridge deck and the upper flight of steps, were fabricated from steel plate – like the Monkwearmouth bridge – forming

Whitby West Cliff Station

The bridge was composed of fabricated steel spandrels on brick bases. The circular details were fabricated, but later cast examples had similar embellishments. The sides to the covered walkway were of wooden construction. (N. Cholmondeley collection)

a curved, flanged girder with ornamental circular panels. Their shape and ornamentation closely mirrored what would become the standard cast design. However, where the later bridges would be mounted on four cast-iron legs under the landings at each side, the West Cliff bridge was mounted on a brick base, incorporating the lower flight of steps and the landing. These bases appear to have been hollow and used as storage, as a door existed in the south side of the structure on the Scarborough platform, which was bricked up at some point prior to closure. This kind of use was common practice on railway stations throughout the area. The bridge was covered – a feature not carried forward onto the later cast version – but this too was a common feature at the time. The sides and roof were of a timber-framed construction, with vertical boarding and cross braces visible on the outside of the lower walls to handrail height. No glazing was provided, but louvered panels gave

A Walk Around Whitby West Cliff Station

The bridge and parachute water tank, soon after closure in 1961. Note the vent in the roof of the ladies' toilet and the gradient board on the platform end. (N. Cholmondeley collection)

ventilation. It is possible that lighting would have been provided from oil burners. The roof was of a sheeted wooden construction, similar to coaching stock roofs, replaced later by curved corrugated sheeting.

Similar bridges were provided south of Scarborough on the Seamer to Hull line and on the William Bell stations of the North Tyne Loop, some of which still exist today. Good examples can be found at Beverley and Cullercoates, retaining the features described; while detail differences are present, both show identical design and constructional elements with the West Cliff bridge. Most readily apparent are the ornate curved roof supports and the timber sides with outside cross bracing. The fabricated spandrels are identical, allowing their flanged construction to be studied.

Locomotive watering facilities were provided at approximately equal distances along the entire route from Saltburn to Scarborough,

Whitby West Cliff Station

A Class D49/2, piloted by an A8 with 'class one' head codes, standing by the parachute tank at the north of the station. This appears to have been a special working, which has generated interest from the enthusiasts on the line side. Note how the six-coach, double-headed set is only just able to fit inside the passing loop. (N. Cholmondeley collection)

at Brotton, Loftus, West Cliff and Robin Hood's Bay. A majority of the trains using the route were hauled by tank locomotives, with limited water supplies, while the difficult nature of the WR&MUR and the S&WR will have reduced their endurance still further.

The NER, like its contemporaries, evolved its own distinctive style of watering columns and tanks, eventually totalling around 650. The first, introduced in the early 1860s, remained the most common. Examples remain in use at Goathland on the North Yorkshire Moors Railway. A

A Walk Around Whitby West Cliff Station

similar, but later style was produced well into the LNER period. In 1883, the year the WR&MUR was completed, the NER introduced parachute columns. This type was used at West Cliff, and two years later, at Robin Hood's Bay. Tanks were provided at the departure ends of both of West Cliff's platforms. The design featured a circular 2,000-gallon tank mounted on a cast-iron column, which incorporated the 8-inch diameter water supply pipe and a heating stove to prevent freezing in cold conditions. A pivoted crane, 10 feet 6 inches above rail level, carrying the bag, was swung out to fill the locomotive tanks. When parachute columns were mounted on platforms, as at West Cliff, drainage was provided via a pedestal basin arrangement. These were also used with the earlier non-parachute water columns. The parachute water column was eventually widely used by the NER, totalling around forty examples. Today, the only survivor in the area is in use at Grosmont, on the North Yorkshire Moors Railway.

The water columns and bridge were removed from West Cliff soon after closure, as the scrap metal they represented had obvious value. The same was true of many steel girder bridges along the route. Stone and brick structures tended to survive much longer, as the cost of their removal was not outweighed by their scrap value.

By the late nineteenth century, the NER had amassed a wide range of station furniture and fittings. It was through the network-wide use of standard items such as barrows, benches, lamps, signage, and, most significantly, colour schemes, that the NER was able to stamp its identity onto its stations. They made wide use of signage at stations and depots, with a high degree of standardisation evident by the early twentieth century. The NER book of miscellaneous standards (1910) gives detailed specifications for station equipment and colours used.

The signal box name board, of LNER origin and probably dating from the late 1920s. These signs had cast letters on a wooden board and were introduced across the LNER, replacing earlier NER enamelled name boards. The NER names were located on the front wall only, while these LNER replacements were mounted on both gable ends. (P. Hughes)

Whitby West Cliff Station

A Walk Around Whitby West Cliff Station

Above and below: NER enamel signage. The projecting 'Booking Office' sign consists of a pair of enamel plates on a wooden backing in a frame. Woodwork was painted chocolate brown. Many such signs were later painted over in the styles adopted by both the LNER and British Railways. This was common on smaller stations, many of which survived until closure. (P. Hughes)

Opposite: The parachute water tanks employed on the WR&MUR and later the S&WR were introduced by the NER in 1883, but later saw use across the whole network. They did away with the need for a tank house to maintain the head of water. The parachute tanks were removed from West Cliff soon after closure, but this example is still at work on the North Yorkshire Moors Railway at nearby Grosmont. Many parachute tanks drained into pedestal basins similar to those used with the earlier cranes, but this one has a drain set into the platform surface. Note the small stove to prevent freezing in winter. The ladder cage is a twenty-first-century addition to comply with current health and safety rules. (P. Hughes)

Whitby West Cliff Station

A standard design of enamel signage plates in a variety of sizes was adopted, displaying chocolate-brown lettering on a buff background. This lettering was of a sans serif, squared off, upper case pattern, which was also used in a condensed form if space was limited. Enamelled plates were mounted in wooden frames for hanging and larger, wall-mounted signage, while smaller, lozenge-shaped plates were used extensively on doors and screens. Station running-in boards were generally mounted on the approach end of platforms, formed from enamel plates in a heavy wooden frame. These were typically mounted on two or three cast-concrete posts. Stations with longer names often had these boards constructed from more than one enamel plate. The wooden frames were painted chocolate brown, while posts were unpainted. Through the LNER period and, in many cases, well into the British Railways era, these signs were retained, painted over in the new colours and lettering of the current operator. The enamel plates typically carried the name of their manufacturer – Chromo (Wolverhampton), Garnier & Company (London) and Orme Evans (Wolverhampton) being the main suppliers of this equipment. The stations on the WR&MUR gained new wooden running-in boards with painted cast letters in LNER days, which replaced the original NER versions. Signal box name boards in a similar style were also introduced at this time, replacing earlier enamelled examples of NER origin. The NER signal box names were fixed to the front of the building, but the later LNER replacements were typically located on each end.

There was also a standard pattern for poster and timetable boards. These had their own colour scheme: the poster area painted black, with frames in chocolate brown and a heading area, which was red with the company name or NER initials in cream-painted, cast-iron, 3-inch letters. There were two types of these boards, one for inside use and one for outside. They differed in that the inside boards had an ornamental wooden capping. Many such boards survived until the stations closed, often with an additional letter 'L' added to the company initials on the top to read 'LNER' from the mid-1920s onwards. Later, some carried an enamel header plate with the 'British Railways' title on a background in the regional colour. West Cliff seems typical of most stations in its use of such boards and appears to have kept them until closure. Traces of mounting points were visible on external walls prior to redevelopment of the station.

A Walk Around Whitby West Cliff Station

A typical NER poster board, with cast-metal letters on a red-painted header. (P. Hughes)

Station seats used in the Whitby area came in two types, using either a knobbled, 'rustic', leg-bracket casting, or one in the shape of a serpent. Neither of these designs was unique to the NER, as similar benches could be found in municipal use around the country. Although their origin is unclear, it is certain they were a standard off-the-shelf casting, which the NER brought in. Both styles came in standard lengths of 9, 10, 11 and 12 feet, with substantial wooden laths supported over three cast-iron brackets. Following closure, it was common to find former station seats reused around the local area. For example, former station seats still exist in Cloughton (former S&WR) and Goathland, on the Whitby to Malton route, both identifiable by the cut-out in the seat back into which the station name plate was screwed.

Whitby West Cliff Station

The 'rustic'-style station bench, on a backdrop rich in NER and LNER character. The 'Ticket Office' sign is an NER type, repainted into a later style, while the cast seat back plate is typical of LNER stations. Grosmont station is restored to represent the 1950s period (P. Hughes)

The cast-iron seatback station names, now so typical of stations in the North East, were not an original NER feature. These were introduced by the LNER in the mid-1920s. Station names were painted directly onto the seat backs until this time.

Study of the NER standards books shows a wide range of station equipment also existed. *The Barrow Diagram Book* (1907) lists almost one hundred designs. The most common on small and medium-sized stations were sack barrows to diagram 60 and four wheeled barrows to diagram 62 and 63, some typical examples being illustrated. Barrows of these types can be seen in the photographs in use at West Cliff and,

A Walk Around Whitby West Cliff Station

Above and below: Although the larger signs were generally painted over and reused during the LNER period, many of the NER flat enamel door plates were replaced by cast examples, such as these. The popular seat back plates carrying the station name were also introduced at this time. (P. Hughes)

as on other stations, many remained well into the BR period. Barrows for passenger use were painted dark green, while those for goods use tended to be mid-grey. Most carried a cast identification number plate, many of which remained in the BR period. Hence, it can be seen that the NER's influence on their stations lasted much longer than the company itself!

A small, portable weighing machine can be seen on West Cliff's Scarborough-bound platform, under the canopy, in some of the photographs. These were also common on NER stations, originating from Pooley of Wolverhampton, who provided and serviced the larger

Whitby West Cliff Station

An NER sack barrow to Diagram 60 and a wheeled barrow, of Diagram 62. Numerous such barrows remained in use for many years. Note the rectangular cast number plate. (P. Hughes)

A Walk Around Whitby West Cliff Station

This portable platform weighing machine, made by Pooley's, spent its working life at West Cliff and is just visible under the awning on the Scarborough platform in some of the pictures. It can now be seen at Grosmont station, on the North Yorkshire Moors Railway, and as such is the only part of West Cliff station still in railway use. (P. Hughes)

Whitby West Cliff Station

Left and opposite: A pair of NER lamp standards. The one on the right has been modified to carry a gas mantle, while that on the left has the original oil lantern. (P. Hughes)

weighing machine in the goods yard. Although mobile, it is unlikely these machines ever moved far off the platform areas, as they tended to be cumbersome. Following closure, the West Cliff machine passed into the hands of the local council, who for many years occupied part of the site behind the Middlesbrough-bound platform. Here, it was used to weigh scrap lead recovered from buildings and eventually it passed into the care of the North Yorkshire Moors Railway. It is now displayed in appropriate surroundings on Grosmont station. As such, it is probably the only part of West Cliff station still in railway use today.

Platform lighting was originally provided by paraffin-lit lanterns mounted on cast-iron posts. These lanterns were held above the post in a square hoop and could be lifted out for cleaning and repair. The station name was carried on an etched glass strip in the upper part of the front frame. No standards book exists covering station lamp styles. Study of photographs highlights the wide variety of lanterns

A Walk Around Whitby West Cliff Station

and, to a lesser extent, post types used, often in a small geographical area. It is reasonable to conclude that, like the station seats, these may have been bought-in, off-the-shelf items. This is reinforced by the fact that the NER initials do not appear on either the post or the lantern, although occasionally they are found on the hoop that fixes the lantern to the post. It is likely that these hoops were locally manufactured to fit specific lantern types to posts, as some variation existed in lantern size. On some minor stations, the cast-iron standard was substituted by a basic square concrete post, to which the lantern hoop was fixed.

At some point in the 1930s, the lighting at West Cliff was changed to gas, as was the case at many other stations at the time that had access to a town gas supply. Typically, only rural stations retained their paraffin lanterns until closure. The new gas lamp heads were installed on the original cast posts, using curved supports. One cast lamp post, without its head, survived at West Cliff long after closure, apparently used as a clothes line post for the station house, and can be seen standing alone in some of the pictures. Sadly, this lone survivor seems to have disappeared when the station was redeveloped, so the pictures included in this chapter are of identical lamps that survive on stations of the North Yorkshire Moors Railway.

Throughout the NER period, stations were painted in a chocolate brown and buff colour scheme. The exact shades used are unclear, as no colour standardisation existed at the time; paints being mixed by eye from reference samples. Hence, some degree of variation will have existed, even between buildings on the same station painted at different times. Study of monochrome photographs indicates that the brown colour was applied to the lower parts of wooden buildings to around window sill level and to guttering, drainpipes, doors and window frames. It was also found on lamp posts and heads, footbridges, platform benches, water tanks and water cranes. The upper parts of wooden buildings, window sashes, weather boards and barge boards were typically finished in buff. The best indication of colours actually used can be found in the study of surviving enamel signage, as the colour of the enamel is not prone to weather in the same way as paint does. Towards the end of the NER period, the buff colour appears to have been used more, but again much variation existed from station to station. While no colour images exist from the NER period, the nature of the colours applied can be understood from the black-and-white photographs.

Following the grouping in 1923, the LNER perpetuated the NER brown and buff colours and signage styles for well over a decade, before adopting the familiar two-tone green and sand colours, which were slowly applied to most stations though the 1930s. The LNER green appears to have survived well into the 1950s at West Cliff.

The graphic designer Eric Gill was engaged by the LNER to create what would now be termed a 'corporate image' for the company in 1929, adopting Gill Sans as his typeface. This was used extensively by the LNER, quickly applied to all company signage and paperwork, as well as on the branding of the Silver Jubilee train in 1935. Its use was perpetuated by British Railways after the Second World War in their national branding of the rail network. Indeed, well into the twenty-first century, Railtrack has used this typeface in its logo, which has now become strongly associated with railway use in the minds of the British public.

A Walk Around Whitby West Cliff Station

Typical NER and LNER station furniture abounds in this view of an autocar set preparing to leave West Cliff for Scarborough in the late 1920s. (N. Cholmondeley collection)

Much NER signage was repainted into these new colours – white Gill Sans capitals on black background with white border – rather than replacing still-serviceable existing signage during the LNER period. This was common on smaller stations. Indeed, many retained their NER signage, reused in this way, until closure. The NER enamel lozenge plates, used on doors and screens, were also repainted. However, on many stations these were replaced by the slimmer cast-iron versions, introduced in the mid-1920s by the LNER. These were in a similar style to the popular cast-iron seat back plates.

With nationalisation in 1947, a similar approach to the early grouping period was followed in that British Railways maintained the regional colour schemes and identities of its stations, while slowly adopting the Gill Sans typeface nationwide. This was ultimately incorporated in the classic British Railways totem logo.

The difficult economic times of the late 1940s and the generally poor state of the rail network meant that for some time the new nationalised

Whitby West Cliff Station

A typical NER running-in board, repainted into the colours of British Railways North Eastern Region. The concrete flower tubs were introduced by the LNER, finding their way in great numbers onto every station on their network. Note also the datum post. (P. Hughes)

A Walk Around Whitby West Cliff Station

railway had more important issues to address than a widespread repaint and rebranding of its infrastructure. When it finally did come in 1952, the Gill Sans typeface was adopted, with network-wide use of the totem logo for smaller station name signs and other applications. A range of standard enamelled signage was created, using white Gill Sans on a coloured background, which was unique to each geographical region. This regional branding was also applied to the station buildings and other infrastructure, by use of colour schemes, which were applied consistently to all railway buildings within the geographic regions. In practice, study of photographs shows that some variation in its interpretation still existed between stations.

In the case of North Eastern Region, the colours used were oriental blue and silver birch, with white window sashes. This in itself reflected the increased range of paint colours available in this period, especially in lighter and bright colours. Before the war, paint pigments were less advanced, leading to colours generally being restricted to more subdued shades. The oriental blue was applied to station buildings in approximately the same areas as the NER brown had been found, with silver birch replacing buff for upper parts of wooden buildings. Tangerine was adopted as the background for North Eastern Region signage, found on repaints of earlier signs and on the new enamel examples. With access to colour photography becoming more widespread around this time, we are fortunate today in that a wide resource of images documenting this period in our railway history exists. Photographs dating from just prior to closure illustrate the blue paintwork and tangerine signage in use at West Cliff. It is possible the station was repainted around the time the WR&MUR was closed.

Prior to the site's redevelopment as housing in 2001, study of the building on the Middlesbrough-bound platform revealed clear traces of all the three colour schemes applied to the station. Of particular interest was a very fresh sample of NER chocolate brown, which has been covered by a metal bracket. This protected and unweathered example appeared as a deep maroon. Samples from the inside of this building showed a pale green, which was widely used on interiors in the BR period and has since been replicated by the North Yorkshire Moors Railway at Grosmont station. Much of the information for colours from the BR period and the nature of their application used in the repainting of Grosmont to 1950s standard were gained from study of the surviving West Cliff buildings.

End of the Line

The run-down of West Cliff station began on 15 May 1958, with the closure of the WR&MUR as a through route. At this time, the signalling was altered to allow the station to function as a terminus. This seems a curious and expensive decision at this late stage as, with the increasing use of DMU stock on the local services, the need to run sets round to reverse direction was greatly reduced. The DMU sets were actually introduced on the day the WR&MUR closed, at the start of the 1958 summer timetable, and will have been in use before this work was completed. In fact, it would have been possible to simplify the layout further and reduce costs without impacting on the operation of the station. After the severing of the WR&MUR, the Whitby Town to Scarborough trains called at West Cliff only to change direction, the vast majority being formed from the new DMU stock. The goods and coal yard was served by the Malton pick-up, but by far the majority of the goods traffic for Whitby was handled at the Town station.

Following complete closure on 10 May 1961, the principal station staff found themselves transferred to Whitby Town. The footbridge, water tanks and signalling equipment were removed soon after closure, presumably because of the scrap metal value of these items. However, the track remained *in situ* with all points disconnected until 1963, although a removable stop block had been installed north of Prospect Hill Junction. The remaining track from here to the buffers at Upgang Lane fell into the hands of the District Engineer on 11 May 1961, being referred to by the local railwaymen as 'The Dead Line'. The Whitby to Scarborough DMUs changed direction at Prospect Hill Junction after this time, just under three quarters of a mile south of West Cliff. The S&WR itself closed in March 1965 under the Beeching

End of the Line

Above and below: All the station buildings remain intact in these immediately post-closure views from the mid-1960s. The bridge and water tanks were removed soon after closure as their scrap metal had obvious value. (N. Cholmondeley collection)

Report, along with the Malton line south of Grosmont Junction, which ultimately became the North Yorkshire Moors Railway. After this time, the Middlesbrough route via the Esk Valley became Whitby's only remaining railway link. This line remains in use today.

The West Cliff station buildings remained empty until around 1970, when they passed into the hands of Yorkshire Water, who used them as offices, with part of the platform area as a storage yard. Part of the canopy on the main station building was enclosed behind metal sheeting to create secure storage, but the canopy itself remained intact behind this. The front of the waiting building on the other side was similarly enclosed, with the glazed wooden screens also remaining unaltered behind. The station house became a council house, as did many other former railway houses in the area.

Over the next few years, most of the site passed into industrial use. The trackbed through the platforms was filled in and used by the Water Board for storage. The Abattoir Bridge arch was bricked up – blocking the trackbed at the north end – and the Stakesby Vale road bridge was demolished in 1967, allowing the road to be widened. This effectively closed the site off at both ends. Access to the main station building and station house was from Station Avenue and the former goods yard, but the track and platform area, which had by this time been fenced off, could only be reached from the Water Board's offices. A footpath, closely following the right of way over the former footbridge, ran along this fence, linking the estates on both sides for pedestrians.

A council yard on the site of the Co-op Creamery, behind the Middlesbrough platform, was accessed through the Stakesby Vale gate. Part of the goods yard and the goods shed were occupied by a builder, who altered the goods shed by the addition of a mezzanine floor and enclosed the loading dock, while the coal cells fell into disrepair. Over the years, many of the large stone blocks seem to have been removed, probably to be reused in building elsewhere.

During this time, apart from the enclosure of the site, little was done to alter the appearance of the remaining buildings. When the Water Board finally vacated the site in the early 1990s, much of the original station remained, including a lamp post, the canopy on the main building and the glazed wooden screens on the Middlesbrough platform building. Much of the interior of this waiting building had been covered by shelving and racking, which was stripped out by vandals over the

End of the Line

The waiting rooms on the Middlesbrough-bound platform around 1997. Behind the wooden lean-to structures, many of the original railway features survived. (P. Hughes)

This fireplace survived inside the enclosed waiting area. (P. Hughes)

Whitby West Cliff Station

The bay platform after the Water Board had moved in, with the cars on the right standing on the main line trackbed. (A. Brown/N. Cholmondeley collection)

The awning survives, partly obscured by the sheet metal structure in this mid-1990s picture. A new corrugated sheet roof has been put on the remaining section of the awning during the Water Board's stay at the station. The stationmaster's house has gained a satellite dish and was still occupied as a council house at this time. (A. Brown/N. Cholmondeley collection)

End of the Line

The Station Avenue side of the main building had changed little by the mid-1990s. The goods shed is in the background. The bricked-up window was to protect the modesty of ladies using the toilet in the south cross-wing. (A. Brown/N. Cholmondeley collection)

The stationmaster's house in the 1990s. Note the lamp post in the yard, which has been used to hang a washing line. (M. Dyson)

Whitby West Cliff Station

The booking hall pavilion in Yorkshire Water days. (N. Cholmondeley collection)

The south cross-wing shortly after Yorkshire Water had moved out. Compare this overgrown, semi-derelict view with that of today. (P. Hughes)

End of the Line

The ladies' waiting room area in 1997. The roof ventilator had been removed by this time. The boarded-up window on the right once looked into an enclosed yard. (P. Hughes)

next few years to expose the bench seating, woodwork and interior details including a pot-bellied stove, all preserved underneath. The stationmaster's house remained in the hands of the Council.

The whole site was purchased for redevelopment as modern housing in 2001. This major work retained the two main surviving station buildings, but the goods shed was lost. This leaves Staithes as the only surviving goods shed on the former WR&MUR. The goods yard and trackbed as far as the Abattoir Bridge were built over and the two remaining station structures converted into flats and houses. It is significant to note that in so doing, the modern-day architect has shown

Whitby West Cliff Station

Today, dormer windows stand in the Booking Hall pavilion roof. Note the new uPVC windows, closely matching the pattern of the originals. (P. Hughes)

The trackbed is now a road and cars take shelter in the waiting room. The new building on the right mirrors the stationmaster's house. Note the pitch of the roof and the window details, taking more than a little of their inspiration from the work of William Bell. The former open waiting area on the left has been filled in with blue brick details. (P. Hughes)

End of the Line

A look down the platforms in the twenty-first century. The cast columns from the awning remain and the south wing block has gained an extra storey. (P. Hughes)

The Abattoir Bridge today. The bridge is no longer a thoroughfare, giving a home for garden buildings spilling over from nearby houses that have been built since the station closed. The bridge arch is closed off with wire fencing, not clearly visible in this picture. (P. Hughes)

Whitby West Cliff Station

Upgang Lane Bridge, looking north where the WR&MUR was severed in 1958. Buffers were erected approximately where the photographer is stood and the track northwards taken up. The mound of earth across the trackbed beyond the span carries a road into a small housing estate. The cutting behind the photographer, leading back to the station, has been partly filled in by the local authority and is now in recreational use. (P. Hughes)

more than a close similarity to the style of William Bell, particularly in the conversion of the former station buildings themselves. The station house on the north end of the main building is now mirrored by a near-identical new build on the opposite side of the trackbed, while a second storey has been added to the south cross-wing. On the platform, the columns for the canopy have been retained, although the canopy itself was removed. The long waiting room on the Middlesbrough platform has lost its attractive, glazed wooden front screens, and the space in the former waiting area is now used for covered car parking, while the brick wing blocks at the ends have gained second floors and dormer windows, becoming flats. All of this fits quite comfortably with the original architecture. A road occupies the in-filled platform area between these two buildings.

End of the Line

A final look over the shoulder down Station Avenue. (P. Hughes)

    The new build work on the site reflects the original station architecture, in the use of blue brick detailing courses and stone lintels. The station area has now been transformed from a collection of increasingly run-down industrial buildings into an attractive residential area. The only negative aspect is that in building so extensively over the goods yard and trackbed, the original building's identity as a former station has been somewhat lost. With the trackbed so completely built over now, there will be no possibility of the route reopening as a railway, although this has never been seriously considered since closure. Railway historians may raise an eyebrow at the choice of name for the development – Beeching Mews – as West Cliff station actually closed a full three years before the controversial secretary of state published his infamous 'Reshaping of British Railways' report. However, his name will always be associated with closed railways and stations in the minds of the British public.

    The final photographs in this chapter take us around the site today. While the railway enthusiast may look back with fondness on the station

Whitby West Cliff Station

of the past, the fact remains that as a structure, West Cliff station has now long outlasted the railway it was built to serve, evolving to fulfil new roles while preserving much of the character of William Bell's style of architecture. Indeed, it could be argued that over a century later, Bell's influence is still strongly felt in the new builds on the site. It is highly probable that in this present incarnation, the remaining station buildings will survive for many decades to come. In a nation rich in history and innovation, the railways that once snaked through almost every town are now another chapter of our social history, that lives on in street names.

Sources

Addyman, J., Foster, C., Hoole, K., Los, A., Mackay, N., Prattley, R., Proud, J., and Richardson, R. (1988). *North Eastern Record (Vol. 1)*. Shears and Sons, Bassingstoke.

Bairstow, M. (1988). *Railways Around Whitby (Vol. 1)*. Foundation Chambers, Huddersfield.

Bairstow, M. (1996). *Railways Around Whitby (Vol. 2)*. Foundation Chambers, Huddersfield.

Fawcett, B. (2001). *A History of North Eastern Railway Architecture (Vol. 1)*. North Eastern Railway Association.

Fawcett, B. (2004). *A History of North Eastern Railway Architecture (Vol. 2)*. North Eastern Railway Association.

Fawcett, B. (2005). *A History of North Eastern Railway Architecture (Vol. 3)*. North Eastern Railway Association.

Hitches, M. (2009). *Steam Around Scarborough*. Amberley, Stroud, Gloucestershire.

Hoole, K. (1985). *North Eastern Branch Line Termini*. Oxford Publishing, Oxford.

Hoole, K. (1994) *The Whitby, Redcar and Middlesbrough Union Railway*. Hendon Publishing, Nelson, Lancashire.

Stamp, C. (2005). *George Hudson and Whitby*. Caedamon, Whitby.

Williamson, D. (2003). *Station Plans: Scarborough – Whitby – Saltburn and Pickering – Seamer*. North Eastern Railway Association.

Acknowledgements

Thanks must go to:

John Alsop, Dave Blackwell, the late John Boyes, Alan Brown, John Bruce, Terry Cartlidge, Neil Cholmondeley, Richard Coates, Mark Dyson, Dave Fenny, the late Tony Goodall, Jonathon Lloyd, The Ken Hoole Study Centre and the staff of the North Yorkshire Moors Railway.

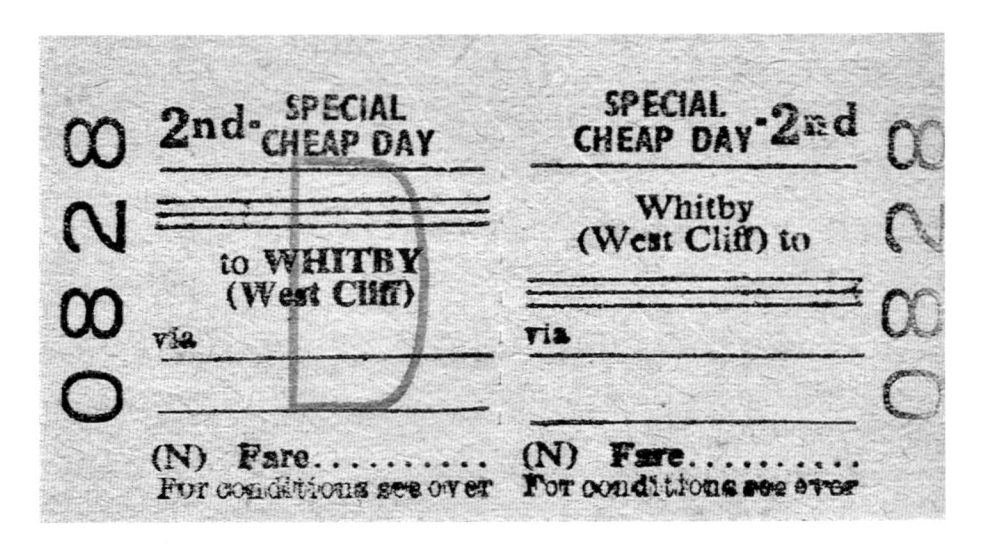

An unstamped Edmondson ticket, from the British Railways era. (P. Hughes)